Seven Days
OF
Solitude

*A Guidebook
for a Personal Retreat*

BROTHER RAMON, SSF

FOREWORD BY JOYCE HUGGETT

ILLUSTRATIONS BY MOLLY DOWELL

Liguori
LIGUORI, MISSOURI

Published by Liguori Publications
Liguori, Missouri
http://www.liguori.org

British edition published by Marshall Pickering, London.

Library of Congress Cataloging-in-Publication Data

Ramon, Brother, SSF.
    Seven days of solitude : a guide to a personal retreat / Brother Ramon ; illustrations by Molly Dowell.—1st U.S. ed.
        p.   cm.
    ISBN 0-7648-0501-0 (pbk.)
    1. Retreats—Episcopal Church. I. Title.

BV5068.R4 R36 2000
269'.6—dc21   99–088234

Printed in the United States of America
First U.S. Edition 2000
04 03 02 01 00   5 4 3 2 1

For Jayne Livingstone (nee Lloyd)
whose joyful friendship I have shared
from her childhood,
and who fed me
with food and humor during
the writing of this book.

Contents

Foreword

I HAVE IN MY POSSESSION quite a collection of letters from prayerful people. Many of them have written to me seeking guidance about where and when to have a Quiet Day or a longer retreat, and how best to use this precious time which they have earmarked for deepening their relationship to God. At last, here is a book I can place into your hands.

Although *Seven Days of Solitude* assumes that a person can carve out one whole week to go away with God and that they will have at their disposal a quiet place in the country-side where they can structure their day as they please, the material could easily be adapted by those who can only snatch a few hours with God in the city or suburbia. The book could further be adapted by groups spending a Quiet Day together.

I write this with confidence, because I have used some of the material on the Away Days I enjoy in a quiet, country cottage and for half-days of prayer in my city-center home and my own prayer life has been enriched by it. Some of the prayers have moved me so deeply that I have wanted to make them my own. Some of the meditations and exercises have challenged me to change my lifestyle; to make it more simple; to make sure that I can be more available to God and to people. And I have loved rising to the further challenge to learn to cook contemplatively! My family and I have enjoyed all of Brother Ramon's recipes though, acutely conscious as I am of the value of a low-fat diet, I have reduced drastically the fat content of most of the meals.

I count it a privilege to recommend this imaginative, timely do-it-yourself retreat guide which flows from Brother Ramon's own ever-deepening relationship with God. In the future, when people write to ask me how to plan a Quiet Day or a private retreat, I shall mention *Seven Days of Solitude* emphasizing that timeless piece of advice: "Pray as you can, not as you can't." Be selective. If it helps to work your way through the book systematically, splendid. If it helps simply to dip and adapt, that is equally valuable. I shall also remind such potential readers of the plus factor of using this book: the assurance that, though our retreat giver is God, while using this book we have the prayer backing of the author—a bonus indeed.

JOYCE HUGGETT

Seven Days

OF

Solitude

PART I

MAKING YOUR RETREAT

Making Your Retreat

I LIKE THE TERM *MAKING A RETREAT* because it gives me a sense of weaving a pattern, creating a work of art, or turning a piece of pottery. I get that feeling sometimes when sharing in a beautifully rendered psalm in plainsong chant—what the psalter calls "praising the Lord in a well-wrought psalm." These are the images I have of making a retreat.

This book is a do-it-yourself guide to making a retreat. You can take it with you to a monastic house, a secluded vacation spot, a cottage, or any place where you can find quiet. It is written with a seven-day personal retreat in mind, but it can be adapted to three-and-a-half days, or be used with a retreat conductor sharing and expounding the themes with some group participation. But I have in mind some solitude in which God can speak and act within your own life.

Although this book communicates the main threads and themes of the pattern, what will emerge from such a retreat will depend on the retreatant's level and measure of participation. I just stopped myself from using the words *intensity of participation*, because *intensity* is the one word I would avoid in this context. What God's people need is not an intense or frenetic approach, producing strain and stress, but a certain passivity of spirit in waiting on God. It is his inspiration we are after, not our perspiration. After all, it is *his* work.

Since writing this book, I have given up my work at Glasshampton Monastery in Worcestershire after six years of receiving retreatants. It has been a great joy to receive Christians from both catholic and evangelical sections of the faith—Quakers, Roman Catholics, Baptists, and Pentecostals—all sharing in Anglican Franciscan liturgy and silence.

Over the last two decades, the retreat movement has been attracting more Christians irrespective of their backgrounds, and my own experience during that time has been a liberation from denominational partisanship into the freedom of sharing fellowship with Christians of all kinds.

This has taken place in cathedral and university contexts, in evangelistic and ministry missions, conferences, and prayer schools, but especially in the conducting of group and personal retreats.

By the time this book is published, I shall be exploring the hermit tradition, which has sounded consistently and increasingly within me for many years. This book encourages *you* to capture something of the amazing solitude in which God can move in your heart by his Spirit.

I am not encouraging individualism for I believe in a healthy, corporate, sacramental, and social Christian life. But unless you face the pain and joy of your own solitude and loneliness, then rushing about from one church group to another will become an evasion of the living God. Of course, we need one another, but our primary task is to discover God within. And from that fertile source and root, fruitfulness and abundance will abound.

What Is a Retreat?

The term does not mean running from the difficulties and responsibilities of life, but rather withdrawing from their immediate and insistent claims in order to be totally available to God. This calls for a certain passivity, receptivity, and "letting go," in a place of comparative solitude and silence, so that the interior Word may be heard in the depths of your being.

For some, this can be accomplished simply with Scripture and silence, though most of us need a bit more input in terms of study, work, and exercise. I well remember the first time I felt a powerful pull toward a two-week period of solitude in a remote cottage on the North Devon coast of England, when I was about twenty-four years of age. I was well used to periods of solitude in small doses for it was natural to my childhood, but I had never had a long period without human contact and it seemed that I was jumping in at the deep end.

This proved to be an immense time of creative awareness for me, though it was a fearful time of facing my own loneliness and pain. I had no help or input from anyone else, but the saving grace was that I was answering an inward call to get away from the demands of an active and enthusiastic pastoral assignment—in order to face myself. It is better to have the guidance of a soul-friend or spiritual director, but not absolutely essential. The Holy Spirit is the ultimate Guide and Director of souls.

These two weeks plunged me into the darkness and loneliness I needed in order to be cast onto the grace and mercy of God. So your time of retreat will cast you on to God if you take your retreat seriously—though not too piously! There is joy in penitence, and the light shines more clearly in darkness.

Retreat, therefore, is a withdrawal from the noise and demands of ordinary, busy life to make time for God in interior stillness. It will involve times of darkness and perplexity, but that is only a clearing of the ground for illumination and some measure of closer and intimate fellowship and love in God. And this, in turn, will overflow in loving and practical compassion for others.

The making of a retreat is nothing new, for apart from its roots in the biblical tradition, it is the universal practice of the ancient faiths, and the contemplative attitude is as old as humankind itself.

There are different kinds of retreats. The traditional form is a conducted, preached retreat in which a group of people come together for some days of quiet reflection, led by a conductor who provides the input within the context of eucharistic or liturgical worship. Such a retreat may be closed (parish, college, intimate group) or open (anyone) and will provide for personal counseling, interviews, and sharing. A silent retreat usually provides times of talking at the beginning and end, and some retreats encourage periods of group sharing.

There are fasting retreats, though normally food is taken in silence, sometimes with readings or music. Some retreats include a certain amount of group participation, learning, along with the techniques of meditation, calligraphy, painting, poetry, or other crafts—all of which may direct the retreatant to a deeper experience of God through such creativity.

There are also journaling retreats in which the retreatant is instructed in the keeping of a spiritual journal, reviewing the past, and looking to future growth but with emphasis on living in the present moment of the Holy Spirit indwelling. Such a journal is useful as you track your journey, hold dialogue with God, and share such writing in confidence with the retreat conductor or soul-friend.

There are retreats devoted to potential soul-friends, healers, counselors, and listeners, often including the healing dimension in its widest sense, with charismatic or sacramental laying-on of hands offered as a ministry, linked with sacramental confession and the Eucharist.

As the retreat movement has spread, new forms are springing up, such as home retreats (one day or evening a week), family retreats (including child-care assistance), day retreats, and drop-in retreats, but this book is mainly concerned with a personal retreat, providing the pattern, timetable, and input required. It does not presume a corporate liturgical provision, though if the retreatant stays at a monastic/retreat house such daily worship can be incorporated with some alteration to the timetable.

The structure of a personal retreat is given in the next section and includes the preparation, cooking, and eating of a simple vegetarian meal. This is not obligatory, of course, for it must be done in the simple and gentle concentration known as *mindfulness*; and for some unpracticed people this could be a source of distraction or frustration—the opposite of what is intended! I find the whole process of preparing and eating such a meal a vital part of my spiritual life, as fasting can be on other days—but this is after much practice!

Problems

Difficulties may well arise. But if they are met with an open and relaxed attitude they can contribute to a good retreat. When I say "open and relaxed," such an attitude must be learned and nurtured. Moving from a busy and organized routine into silence and solitude can be a shock to the system. There is need to unwind physically, mentally, and spiritually.

The human person is a unity, but it is useful to think of ourselves in this threefold manner as long as we do not get involved in a dualism of separation. Saint Paul prays for the Thessalonian believers: "May the God of peace make you holy through and through, and keep you sound in spirit *(pneuma),* soul *(psyche),* and body *(soma),* without fault when our Lord Jesus Christ comes." Then he adds for good measure: "He who calls you is to be trusted and he will do it!"

If this is the foundation of our spirituality, then problems are on the way to being solved. The word *psychosomatic* indicates the bridging of mind *(psyche)* and body *(soma),* and in the use of such a word the medical world now takes full notice of the linking of health and disease in the whole person. The Christian also experiences the opening up of a fuller, deeper dimension of spirit *(pneuma),* by which is meant that dimension of the human person which experiences God in true inwardness and relatedness. If this is understood, then the problems mentioned in this section can be transformed into positive blessings. For instance, difficulties in concentration, distractions, and an anxious and worrying disposition may be helped in a relaxation method of quiet and controlled breathing. The technique of *centering* is an aid here and will be introduced in the next section.

Depression is another problem. I'm not talking about pathological depression. Such people should not go on retreat without careful consultation and counsel. But all people experience forms of depression sometimes, and a sudden confrontation with solitude and silence may well bring dark fears to the surface. The retreatant must be patient, relaxed, open, and welcoming of changes of mood and temper—it is all grist to the mill and can lead us into a deeper knowledge of ourselves and an experience of the grace, mercy, and compassion of God.

Sometimes in solitude, instead of the expected "peace that passes understanding" there may arise powerful emotions that have not been allowed expression in our busy and repressed daily lives. With normal pressures removed and respectable facades made unnecessary, there may arise a surge of anger, grief, depression, resentment—or joy! These may be accompanied by tears, laughter, trembling, or breathless wonder. Of course, such an introduction to our deeper self— our real self—may bring immense relief or else feelings of guilt or fear, indicating the need for counsel, sacramental confession, and inner healing.

The spirit of openness and relaxation mentioned above will give us the quiet honesty and integrity to face all this. The fact is that when I come with sincerity of heart, a certain physical passivity, and an open spirit exposed to the divine presence, then the door to my profound and unconscious self is left open, and there wells up into my conscious being those depths that are usually hidden or repressed.

There may be an inflow of love, joy, and peace, or of repressed fears, violence, and guilt—or even the erotic fantasies which my policing conscience does not allow to surface in my normal conscious life. This can be most unwelcome in times of retreat or periods dedicated to contemplative prayer! Nevertheless it is good for my soul and works toward my ultimate healing and salvation.

Biblical Basis

There is a firm biblical foundation for making a retreat. Whenever God took his people forward into a new chapter of experience, he called a man or woman into the desert, mountain, wilderness, or into interior silence—calling, convicting, renewing, and transforming him or her to become a bearer of his word and power to the community and to the surrounding peoples. I shall just list some of them, but it would be worthwhile studying each of the references carefully:

- Abraham's vision and intercession at Mamre (Gen 15,18)
- Jacob's vision at Bethel (Gen 28:10–17)
- Jacob's wrestling with the angel (Gen 32:22–32)
- Joseph's youthful dreams (Gen 37:1–11)
- Joseph's growing discernment in prison (Gen 39:20; 41:40)
- Moses at the burning bush (Ex 3:1–18)
- Moses on Mount Sinai (Ex 33:18–23; 34:29–35)
- Elijah in retreat at Cherith (1 Kings 17:1–7)
- Elijah in flight to Horeb (1 Kings 19:1–13)

- John the Baptist's first thirty years
  (Lk 1:5–25, 57-80)
- John's imprisonment and martyrdom
  (Mk 6:21–29)
- The interior life of Mary (Lk 1:26–56; 2:22–52;
  Jn 19:25–27)
- Saul's conversion and retreat into Arabia (Acts
  9:1–19; Gal 1:11–24)
- John the Divine on the isle of Patmos
  (Rev 1:9–10)

Apart from all the above biblical testimony there is the life of Jesus himself. He treasured a hidden, interior, contemplative life, dwelling continually in the Holy Spirit and in the love of his Father. Nevertheless, he constantly went into the wilderness, into desert places, climbing up the mountain, often spending all night in prayer and communion with God. He didn't take a prayer book with him. Rather, on the mountain, in the solitary places, and in the Garden of Gethsemane, he offered up loud cries and tears in adoration, intercession, and inexpressible groanings.

The Pattern of Jesus

If we take Jesus as our example, we can trace at least four reasons why he withdrew into silent and communion with the Father:

1. To dwell within the divine Love
2. To be filled with the Spirit for conflict with dark
   powers

3. For guidance and direction
4. For physical, mental, and spiritual refreshment
   and renewal

If he needed to do so in his humanity, how much more do we?

I am not suggesting that when you go into retreat you will be swept into ecstasies of vision, or into direct and immediate conflict with dark cosmic powers. These are the fruit of a lifetime's discipline and discipleship. But you have to begin somewhere—and spending time alone with God in retreat may be God's next step for you.

The order in which Jesus' retreat into solitude is presented here has to be inverted for us in our experience. Let's look at the four reasons for retreat from our vantage point.

1. We need physical rest and relaxation from the frenetic activity of our busy lives. Part of Elijah's problem at Horeb was that he was physically exhausted—that's why the angel of the Lord gave him food and caused him to sleep! There is a place for fasting from food and sleep, but that is much further along the journey.

Then there is psychological retreat from the busy world of work, confrontation, and upwardly mobile success. A friend of mine recently declined the offer of an assignment which would put him on the road to becoming a bishop. Another friend is taking early retirement at the age of fifty-four to be simpler in his lifestyle and more available to God and to people. A retreat allows us to do this—at least for a time.

The human *psyche* is beset by conscious and (still more)

unconscious problems and needs to be put into neutral gear during a time of retreat. The need is to unwind—and then to be open, quiet, gentle, reflective, passive—and that brings us to the borderland of the spiritual. Of course, the spiritual includes the physical and the mental, but if we think of that tripartite division we mentioned earlier, then the *spirit* indicates that profound depth which longs and yearns for God and which is the "holy of holies" where the *Shekinah*, the radiant glory of the Holy Spirit, dwells.

Making a retreat is an art, of course, but the wonderful thing is that there is a beginner's joy in it. The Lord is gracious because he often pours immense joy into one's first retreat—but that is usually a bait to catch a fish. I mean that once one is hooked, there are hard times ahead. I'm not now referring to the awful confrontations with dark powers— that is for the higher levels of the mountain. I mean that there is one's own emptiness, bankruptcy, boredom, restlessness, and downright sinfulness to deal with!

I well remember, when I first experimented with the religious life, how Father Roland Walls led me up to a tiny hut in the Pentland Hills of Scotland. The hut was dedicated to Saint Seraphim of Sarov and his icon was on the inside of the hut. I asked Father Roland why it was not displayed on the outside, and he gave me a salutary answer with a twinkle in his eye: "The King's daughter is all-glorious *within*." He also said, "The next smallest dwelling for you will be your coffin!" And on our first meeting he left me at my hut, saying, "You must learn to be completely bored with yourself in order to be cast upon God." All these were lessons which I have had to learn. But the beginning is with physical, mental, and spiritual refreshment, leading to renewal.

2. The second reason for retreat is for guidance and direction. It has been a joy to help different kinds of people in retreat at Glasshampton toward a new direction in their lives. For some it has meant a marriage or a new job. For others it has been coming to terms with a broken relationship, bearing the burden of rejection or the taking up of new challenges and responsibilities. If Jesus needed times of solitary seclusion on the mountain, in the wilderness, away from demanding crowds and disciples, so do we.

The very nature of retreat emphasizes the fact that we do not have to demand, harass, and cajole God to show us his will. He is not reluctant and we do not have to take the initiative. He is well able to reveal his will according to his own time and pattern. But we need to *be there*, with an openness and passivity that says, "Here I am, Lord." I notice that it is often evangelical Christians who are most restless and impatient to know "What? Where? When? How? Why?"—sometimes accompanied by the insistent demand "Now!" This is an observation more than a judgment, and to balance that observation let me say that some Catholic-minded Christians need an evangelical firecracker behind them!

3. Third, there are such things as dark powers. They are both psychological and cosmic—I mean both subjective and objective. There is a middle way to tread here, for I find the need to steer carefully between those who see demons everywhere and those who construct a theology which demythologizes the dark powers of the New Testament into the thought-forms of an archaic culture. There is no doubt in the minds of those who enter the hermit tradition that the

pressure of darkness upon the human *psyche* both comes from within *and* invades from an objective and cosmic dimension without.

When Jesus was baptized and filled with the Holy Spirit at the Jordan, then he was both led (Mt 4:1) and driven (Mk 1:12) by the same Spirit into the wilderness. There followed a long period of fasting, reflection, communion with God, and wrestling with the dark temptations of Satan within the depths of his own heart. The redemption of the world was at stake. The issue was momentous and the "Jesus-movement" would have come to an end at his eventual death if he had taken the way of the politician, the economist, or the wonder-worker, as was suggested to him.

Confrontation with dark powers as to the "way" Jesus should take was not the only form of temptation and conflict. Jesus confronted the devil most fully, openly, and completely when he put all the powers of darkness to flight by his mighty death and Resurrection (Heb 2:14; 1 Jn 3:8), making an open spectacle of them and bringing them into captivity and submission (Col 2:15).

There is, of course, a unique sense in which Jesus confronted the dark powers for the redemption of the world—a work which he did *for* us. But there is also that which he does *in* us. We are called to enter into his redemptive work and in his strength and grace to know our own confrontation, sharing the fellowship of his sufferings (Phil 3:10), and by our prayers and love putting dark powers to flight for the good of our world.

That kind of spiritual warfare is open to every Christian (Eph 6:10–12), though few enter such a battlefield. Those who do realize quite soon the need for solitude and waiting upon God, for only the Spirit-filled Christian dare contemplate such a path.

4. Now we come to the primary and basic reason for prayer in solitude. Simply stated, it is for the love of God alone. But such a statement must be unpacked, for it contains many layers of meaning, both open and hidden. I can only hint at its inner meaning because when a lover is asked to give clear and logical reasons for his devotion and adoration of his beloved, he either lapses into silence—and that is a fitting response to such a request—or he stammers incoherently in an attempt to communicate the inwardness of the love which brings him to tears and to the eventual realization that silence is the proper attitude. In my room at Glasshampton I had facing me one of the sayings of Ramon Lull, that Franciscan lover of God: "The Beloved silenced his lover. And the lover received comfort by gazing upon the Beloved."

The primary task of the lover is to enter into union with the Beloved. Words like worship, adoration, contemplation, are appropriate, but even they fall far short of the consummation of union. This is far from the narcissistic navel-gazing of pseudomystics, for the true mystical life overflows in compassion and dynamic energy, and those mystics who are reduced to silence when commanded to describe mystical union in love are the very ones who burst forth in spontaneous adoration of God in poetry and prayer in praise of the ineffable Love which burns in their deepest center.

It was many years before I could read the works of Saint John of the Cross—and don't think you can take a short cut by enthusiastically purchasing his works when you read these

words! When at last I began to read, it was a long time before I realized that I could not expect the exposition of his
fiery poetry to reveal the inward secrets of mystical love.
Much of his exposition clears the ground, exposes evasions,
objections, corrosions, and subterfuges of the soul. And when
at last I found myself devastated with such a poem as *The
Living Flame of Love*, I ran to his explanation of the poem
to draw from the master the essence and center of its meaning—and I was disappointed. The final stanza runs like this:

> *How gently and how lovingly*
> *You lie awake in my bosom*
> *Where alone You secretly dwell;*
> *And in Your sweet breathing*
> *Full of grace and glory*
> *How tenderly You fill me*
> *With Your love.*

I know what that means and, at the same time, I am exas-
perated, restless, and distracted because I do not know! It
would take me many years to enter into the beginnings of
true understanding and experience, so I run to the explanation the saint wrote and find this kind of writing:

> *In that awakening, which is as though one were to
> awaken and breathe, the soul feels a strange delight in
> the breathing of the Holy Spirit in God, in which it is
> sovereignly glorified and taken with love...*

Yes, that confirms that I am on the right track, and now I
expect to find a precise and mystical unfolding of the in-

ward work of the divine Spirit so that my own soul will be caught up into its glory; and I read:

I do not desire to speak of this spiration, filled for the soul with grace and glory and delicate love of God, for I am aware of being incapable of so doing, and were I to try, it might seem less than it is...

and then he finishes the exposition by a string of tantalizing phrases in which he speaks of the enkindling of the divine Love as indescribable and incomprehensible "in the depths of God, to Whom be honor and glory for ever and ever. Amen."

And I am left, as if the Beloved had brought the lover into the glory and ecstasy of yearning love, and then fled into the night, leaving a trail of perfumed glory and light that serves only to inflame the lover's wound still further, causing him to groan with inexpressible longings.

And this brings me to the reason for this book. The last paragraph reveals me as a man living in tension. As one mystical poet puts it: "I suffer, yet I rest"—satisfied with the love of God in Christ, yet restless to enter more deeply, to climb still higher, to be immersed, conjoined, and united in love.

The rest of this book contains counsel, description, meditations, and exercises on the way. It deals with the images of earth and sky of which we have limited experience but which are also icons—or windows into the nature of love and of God.

Some of the material is simple and lowly, but that's where we are. My hope is that you will begin at the beginning, make slow but certain progress; then find yourself ascending, with all the glory and promise that the challenge of an ascending mountain path can impart.

If you "make your retreat," and in the making find it to be a work of love, then my attempt will have been rewarded. For although I cannot describe to you what the divine Love means to me, does to me, promises to me—yet I can show you the map, indicate the way, plant your feet on the lower reaches—and encourage you to climb!

And if you truly begin…then you will catch fire too and you will understand.

PART II

PREPARATION AND METHOD

Preparation
and Method

Contemplation

I USE THE WORD IN THIS CONTEXT *to* mean a contemplative attitude to each day and therefore *to* the week. It is known in the Christian tradition as "living in the present moment" and in other traditions by such words as "mindfulness." The word *contemplation* (Greek *theoria*) has to do with vision and awareness. It is a basic human attitude that most of us have lost but which can be regained by a disciplined openness to ourselves and our environment. It is a basically simple attitude, and at best it needs no instruction—indeed techniques can make it complicated and unnatural! It is to wake up in the morning, to allow oneself to become fully aware of body and mind, and to say: "I awake. May all living beings become awake to love and live in its awareness" and to live through the day in the practice of such awareness.

After habitual practice of meditation, it should become part of one's daily life, imparting strength and quality to all positive action and existing as a reservoir of patience and maturity in times of stress, confrontation, and situations of anger or threat.

It is not meant to be reduced to a religious technique, but because it is no longer natural to many of us, there are various methods of relearning it. The method I commend here is known as *centering down*, and it has as much to do with the preparation, cooking, and eating of the daily vegetarian meal as it has with what we think of as an exposure to the "holy" in meditation on Scripture and prayer.

These are different aspects of the wholeness of life, for nature and grace ought not to be in opposition. They become increasingly compatible in contemplative practice, and the words *growing in grace* carry that expectation.

Structure

Timetable

This is variable, and the inclusion of meal times must be according to the ability of the retreatant, but the following may serve as a guide:

7:00 A.M.	Rise, ablutions
7:30 A.M.	Psalm and meditation
8:00 A.M.	Breakfast
9:00 A.M.	Morning theme: This part of the day includes the Centering Down method, the Scripture reading and meditation provided, and leads to the exercise which follows.
10:30 A.M.	Exercise
12 noon	Meal preparation, cooking, eating, rest

2:00 P.M.	Manual/creative work (carpentry, gardening, calligraphy, bookbinding, painting, and so on)
4:30 P.M.	Coffee or tea break
5:00 P.M.	Evening theme
6:30 P.M.	Exercise
7:30 P.M.	Psalm and meditation
8:00 P.M.	Light repast (optional)
8:30 P.M.	Music (listening or making); reflection on day; journal writing
9.30 P.M.	Compline and retire

Some retreatants will need a great deal of time for meditation and will be able to sit for an hour without any problem. Others will need shorter periods, and some retreatants find the reading of a biography or one of the "great" novels to be part of the interior journey. Advice must be taken on these matters, as in the matter of diet, which we deal with next. Variation among individuals is so great, that what is given here is in terms of guidance only.

Diet

The inclusion of a simple vegetarian meal each day has the purpose of encouraging patience and awareness of our dependence on the earth. The retreatant should adopt an attitude of reflection and mindfulness throughout the whole exercise—while preparing the food, cooking it, eating it, and digesting it! Do not underestimate the importance of such an exercise. The peeling and chopping of an onion in the preparation of a meal can be the place of insight into the interdependence of all living beings within the natural order. This may be the moment of cosmic awareness which will transform your way of seeing—and of living.

A different, but basically simple, recipe is offered each day, none of which needs more than a portable electric skillet or hot plate (you may be retreating in a tent or hut!). One simple meal per day is an exercise in simplicity and discipline, providing a middle way between fasting (which is a wholesome practice in itself) and overeating (which is always to our detriment). But be sensible and don't attempt heroic asceticisms!

Centering Down

This is one of the methods of a contemplative/meditative way of prayer. There are many other methods but this one is simple and effective. The three steps are (1) resting; (2) breathing; (3) opening.

(1) *Resting*   Go to your prayer place; loosen all tight clothing, removing footgear; find your own posture (lying, sitting, prayer stool); let go of all tension in physical relaxation, stretching and relaxing each part of your body, beginning with the soles of your feet and slowly moving upward to the crown of your head—until you are relaxed in body and yet alert in mind. Find your center of stillness in God.

(2) *Breathing*   This second step concerns a simple breathing exercise to bring your respiration into a slightly slower and deeper mode than usual, leading to the breathing of a

prayerful longing in God. First, don't *change* your breathing but *note* its rate and rhythm.

Now gently begin to breathe from the diaphragm instead of from the top of your chest (belly-breathing), and with the deepening, slow it down slightly. Your tummy will rise as you begin such breathing, and as the top of your lungs fill it will lower slightly. After a minute or so of such easy, relaxed breathing find your own level—that is, a level that suits you without strain or effort. The aim here is to let go of all stress and be completely relaxed—no push or effort but simple, easy, passive resting in God.

Now you can begin breathing the prayer—first verbally and then mentally—as you move into its rhythm. Again there are a variety of prayers, including the Jesus Prayer. The prayer offered here is twofold and is breathed within the Triune mystery of God. You need not be concerned with the theology of all this (though it is very powerful), but simply breathe the prayer in loving receptivity, expecting the indwelling of God's Holy Spirit to become the basis and ethos of your meditation. The prayer runs:

> *In You, my Lord, I live*
> > *and move*
> > *and have my being.*
>
> *In me, my Lord,*   *You live*
> > *and move*
> > *and have Your being.*

As you breathe this repetitive prayer, you will enter into its rhythm and yield yourself to the loving mystery of God. Stay there for as long as you want (five minutes is not too short nor thirty minutes too long).

(3) *Opening* You are already open to God, but this word *opening* now indicates your receptiveness to the theme of the session. It is the bridge period of resting in God after the breathing prayer has moved from the mouth to the mind and down into the heart. That is a way of saying that the prayer has become inward and has worked its own purpose of bringing you into the attitude of communion with God, pliable under his inspiration and open to his illumination.

Stay with this opening attitude until you feel ready for the introduction and prayer, which initiates the teaching section of each session. This *centering down* exercise should be practiced at the beginning of each morning and evening session.

Daily Ingredients

The ingredients of the morning and evening sessions with their themes are therefore:

1. Centering Down
2. Introductory paragraphs and prayer
3. Reading of the Scripture passages indicated
4. Perusal of the meditative material
5. Period of silence
6. Exercise

The retreatant is free to incorporate other liturgical or devotional material around the theme, such as sharing in the Eucharist.

Before we begin the main part of the book, with the seven days of themes, there is one important matter I want to explore which we have already mentioned briefly. It is that of mindfulness.

This is a practice which is wider than the Christian tradition and illustrates "living in the present moment." I introduce the practice here, as it is appropriate to reflect upon it before beginning the seven days. But it is worth returning to later or during the retreat, for it will keep body, mind, and spirit centered in the present moment where God is at work.

Mindfulness

I have come to love and treasure this word, for it is one of those "uniting" words that indicate a simple human practice found in all contemplative human beings, though they may not know the word. It means the ability to give oneself wholly to one thing, to one person, to one discipline, and to allow oneself to be caught or taken up into an absorbing pattern of meaning. Perhaps this description sounds like a counsel of perfection, but I find it in Mungo, our monastery dog, when you take a stick, which he longs to carry, or when you take up his lead, which indicates a walk. At such times he sits in complete stillness, fixes you with his beautiful brown and soulful eyes, and holds you with such concentration that he is a "dog of one thing." This is mindfulness.

There are some practices that are not conducive to mindfulness. I suppose I ought to be glad when I see young (and older) people walking along with earpieces or headphones, listening to their favorite music, because I do not then have to be subjected to what might be an invasive cacophony of noise. But the message they seem to give is "Keep your distance! I'm not interested in the world around me, in the life that passes by me and through which I pass. I have my own private world, and you are not invited in."

It used to be the case that the brothers in our monastery did not have personal radios. Then it seemed that music and world events should be part of our life of enjoyment and prayer, so in order not to invade the quiet of the monastery, headphones appeared; but they were used only in private and outside of working hours. Then they began to appear (without permission) in the garden, workshop, laundry, even the sacristy, though not in the kitchen! So we had a problem, for it was difficult to discriminate between places, times, or types of programs—people appreciate Mozart and Heavy Metal at different levels! The only way was to say that they should not be used in public or common places.

The reason is that it is not conducive to mindfulness, for mindfulness is the giving of oneself completely to one thing at a time. The words *distraction, dislocation, preoccupation*, indicate unmindful inattention to the work in hand or to the person who needs your undivided attention.

The Principles of the Society of Saint Francis, speaking of corporate, and especially private, prayer puts it thus:

Praise and prayer constitute the atmosphere in which the brothers and sisters must strive to live. They must endeavor to maintain a constant recollection of the presence of God and of the unseen world. An ever-

deepening devotion to Christ is the hidden source of all their strength and joy...corporate worship is not a substitute for the quiet communion of the individual soul with God, and they must strive to go forward to ever fuller enjoyment of such communion, till they are living in so constant a remembrance of God's presence that they do indeed pray continually.

The practice of mindfulness is not a call to pious aloofness, but rather the opposite. It is to enter into, to enjoy, to absorb, what is immediately before you. I have often felt that we do little justice to the food we eat in our monastery because we read as we eat our silent meals. It would be a better practice of mindfulness if we gave ourselves to the way of eating in quietness and awareness of one another, with full attention to the food before us.

I remember, some years ago, spending a week on retreat at a convent and appreciating in mindfulness the wholesomeness of the home-grown vegetables, convent-made cheese, and fresh milk. While I was there I took a day out and hitched down to a large resort at Barry Island in Wales where my parents were spending a week. I ate with them (prior to my vegetarian diet) in a huge dining area. I stood in the line with my tray and was served a slither of fatty meat between two pieces of plastic, mounds of instant mashed potatoes that still had crumbly powder in them, and tasteless carrots floating in a greasy, watery substance that ran around the gravy—it was better not to practice mindfulness! That was the "real world"—and I had come from the presumably make-believe world of the convent. By their fruits you shall know them!

In this book the concept of mindfulness is illustrated in the preparation and eating of a meal. From this it is clear how the practice may operate in all the good things of life—whether washing the dishes, pruning fruit trees, surfing, playing sports, making music, nursing an elderly person, or making love.

At the beginning of each of the seven days, there is provided a recipe/menu for a simple vegetarian meal. The reason it is there is because it will integrate work, leisure, and pleasure in the necessary acts of preparing, cooking, eating, and digesting a meal in a simplicity that embraces the wholeness of life. This book is not written to promote vegetarianism, but the emphasis away from meat and stimulants also makes the point of simplicity, health, and body-awareness.

If you become aware of what you eat and apply the principle of mindfulness to the gathering, preparation, and cooking of the food, there will be a greater interest and delight in eating it mindfully, without distraction. There will also be the logical extension of thinking of the digestive system and the linking of all this with cleanliness of body and mind and the necessity for gentle exercise.

Mindfulness embraces all these categories, for the body and mind are one. The *psychosomatic* relation of mind and body in the living person is accepted as the only way to relate to oneself and to other people in sickness and in health.

It is not always possible to prepare vegetables that you have grown yourself, but it is well to remember the earth from which they came. We cannot grow enough of our own vegetables in the monastery but when, in season, we dig or gather them, they are, unlike processed or categorized commercial vegetables, dirty, funny-shaped and awkward—but what a difference in taste and flavor!

To chop an onion, peel a turnip, grate a carrot, and scrub a potato can be a great joy. And if done in mindfulness it can be an act of meditation and a source of tranquillity and thankfulness.

This practice of mindfulness is not an act which is put on, or simply a habit which one acquires, but should flow from an inward state of centered tranquillity. And this, in turn, is a gift of the Holy Spirit. You will find in this book, as in my approach to the teaching of meditation, that I do recommend certain methods or techniques of relaxation, concentration, and centeredness, to bring mind and body into a receptive and positive attitude. But one is not saved by techniques or redeemed by methods! The primary thing, in conversion of the heart to God, as in a mindful approach to prayer and life, is to look to the grace of the Holy Spirit, and to see that the eternal Spirit of God moves in the profound depths of the human spirit. At this level grace and the practice of mindfulness are born.

Life's Wholeness

From the foregoing it will be clear that I am affirming a holistic approach to life. The word *psychosomatic*, which we have already used, indicates the relatedness of mind and body, but it goes further than this. I am affirming the relatedness of all living things and of living organisms as rooted in the very stuff of creation. Without accepting all that Fritjof Capra writes, his two major books, *The Tao of Physics* and *The Turning Point*, emphasize the holistic approach to life, and at the end of the former book he writes words which have become strikingly urgent and relevant to the time in which we live:

> *I believe that the world-view implied by modern physics is inconsistent with our present society, which does not reflect the harmonious interrelatedness we observe in nature. To achieve such a state of dynamic balance, a radically different social and economic structure will be needed: a cultural revolution in the true sense of the word. The survival of our whole civilization may depend on whether we can bring about such a change.*

And in the latter book, in his chapter "Wholeness and Health," Capra says:

> *For the past three hundred years our culture has been dominated by the view of the human body as a machine, to be analyzed in terms of its parts. The mind is separated from the body, disease is seen as a malfunctioning of biological mechanisms, and health is defined as the absence of disease. This view is now slowly being eclipsed by a holistic and ecological concept of the world which sees the universe not as a machine but rather as a living system, a view that emphasizes the essential interrelatedness and interdependence of all phenomena and tries to understand nature not only in terms of fundamental structures but in terms of underlying dynamic processes.*

Such an approach is the key to our ecological as well as our moral and spiritual problems because it is the approach of the great spiritualities of the world, including Christianity with its roots in biblical Judaism. If we can begin with a sense of our own wholeness as individuals, we can then move out to our families, friends, communities, and from there see, feel, and experience our relationship and solidarity with the whole human race and our relatedness to all living organisms. This is set within the context of the planet itself and the whole vast cosmic process which is incomprehensible to our finite state but which manifests something of the wonder and mystery of God.

Such a holistic perspective, to be genuine and truly spiritual, must be practical and must increase the amount of love and compassion in the world. If compassion is not present, then it is of no use. Or worse, it may be used to bring others into subservience. As Saint John says: "But whoever hates another believer is in the darkness, walks in the darkness, and does not know the way to go, because the darkness has brought on blindness" (1 Jn 2:11).

So the attitude of mindfulness, set within the context of the wholeness of life, directly affects our relationship with our fellow human beings. When someone comes to me for help, counsel, or spiritual direction, my Christian practice of mindfulness allows me to give myself wholly to that person. First of all I relax with the person in openness of being. Then I listen, with little or no interruption. I receive what is being communicated by the spoken word; in addition, the person's attitude and body language tell me a great deal. All this is within the seal of confidence and in the context of compassion.

Out of such an encounter communication flows, understanding is achieved, and healing springs up. Last week a Baptist minister came to make his first confession, and the healing power that flowed from such an encounter with God and between us was palpable, as his fears were removed, the problems of years were brought out into the open, and a spirit of joyful penitence and forgiveness was experienced.

This can happen not only in a sacramental or religious way but between any two (or more) human beings who allow themselves to be open and trusting to each other, with all the risks that are involved.

Begin It in Me

All that has been said in this introductory chapter has its beginnings in the individual in order for it to flow through you and into other lives. The solitude, the Scripture, the meditations, the exercises, and the practical common round of daily living through the rest of this book during your retreat will integrate all that we have said. Perhaps it is summed up quite simply in John Keble's words:

> *The trivial round, the common task*
> *Will furnish all we ought to ask—*
> *Room to deny ourselves, a road*
> *To bring us daily nearer God.*

PART III

THE SEVEN DAYS

DAY 1

Earth and Seasons

Morning of Day 1: The Earth

We are children of the earth, and we reflect within our lives
the unity of humankind and the diversity which shows itself
in differences of color, language, culture, tradition, and cli-
mate.

Within our own national group there are differences of
genetic inheritance, of educational and cultural background,
and (sadly) of class and financial status. We are also subject
to variation in health and mood, and we carry all this diversity with us in our daily experience as children of earth.

Today, as we begin the first day of our retreat, there are

people for whom such a week of quiet would be a luxury beyond their dreams, and others for whom it would be hell on earth and who would be bursting with frustration after the first hour of solitude.

There are people who have faced this new day singing, and others with terminal illness or manic depression who opened their eyes (if they slept at all) to face another gray day of pain, helplessness, and despair. All these are children of the earth.

If this week of retreat does its work, under God we shall become more aware of our mortal vulnerability as children of the earth, and of our spiritual strength and awareness as children of God. We are both human and divine, and both aspects of our nature should exist in harmonious balance. The experience of earth and heaven is written into our nature; and we begin this morning with our planet Earth.

Prayer

God and Father of all: Your loving energies are at work in the most distant planet and in every cell of my physical body. As I reflect today upon my rootedness in the earth, so let me glimpse something of your glory, and as a child of earth know that my ultimate home is in heaven. Through Jesus Christ, our Lord. Amen.

Scripture Reading

Read the following Scripture passages slowly: Genesis 1:1–5; Psalm 4.

Meditation

On this first morning, the earth is a good place to begin our retreat, for it is the basic place upon which our feet are planted. That which is *planted* implies roots, sustenance, growth, and fruit, and it is a corrective to our modern Western idea of our objective independence to be able to say that we are rooted into the earth and that we draw sustenance and growth from it. We are not separate and independent entities, but there is an interdependence between the earth and humankind.

The name *Adam* means humankind, and its basic meaning is *earth*, the ground, the *humus* from which we come and to which we go. So when we speak about the earth, we speak about ourselves as human beings. Putting it more personally, I speak about myself.

Therefore, the object of our meditation this morning is to *feel* ourselves to be in relationship to the earth. It is necessary today to walk upon the earth, to feel the texture of soil and grass beneath our feet, to take ourselves away from paving stones, concrete, and asphalt, which insulate us from the good earth and give us a false sense of protection from the threat of our own earthiness.

It is not possible for us to take a vantage point away from the earth and evaluate it as an objective outsider. One of the most beautiful pictures of our era is the photograph of our planet taken from space—the astronauts' picture of our world. They found the perspective breathtakingly beautiful, and the first sight of that picture reproduced on earth evoked sheer delight. Never before had we looked upon our world from "out there." And yet those very astronauts were subjectively involved. I'm told that a common feeling among those who have traveled through space over a period of time is a sense of confusion about where they belong. Imagine the awful predicament of a group of earthlings who are stranded in outer space and discover that there is no possibility of ever returning. What would the rest of their lives mean, cut off from mother earth, even if their physical and mental faculties could be perpetuated to a normal life span?

I am writing these words in front of my window at Glasshampton Monastery. There is a light breeze blowing across the lilac bush and chestnut trees outside my window, and I look over the laurel hedge to see, spread out before me on this late July day, a whole field of half-cut golden wheat. The harvester stands silent in the corner, and half a dozen giant rolls of straw lie scattered about the stubble on the cut field. The rest of the wheat moves gently, gracefully under the breeze, with the surrounding green fields of potatoes and sugar beets contrasting in color with the golden field before me.

I don't know whether I communicate the beauty and the sadness of this scene. Beauty, because it is a manifestation *of* the fruitfulness of the good earth, because it displays the earthy glory of fertility and productive growth, and because it reveals a basic aspect of the nature of the Holy Spirit who is the Lord, the Lifegiver. Sadness, because it participates already in the melancholy of harvest, the first suggestion of mellow autumn fruitfulness.

The linking of the earth with fecundity, nurture, and growth makes clear why we use the term "mother earth." The womb is the beginning of our life. It is the seed-receiving, warm, embracing center of fertility, and the language of maternity, fertility, and nurture engenders feelings of warmth, security, and assurance.

None of this indicates a frightened and fleeing return to the womb from a challenging and demanding world, but rather an acknowledgment of our origins, a complete acceptance of our earthiness, our sexuality, our belonging to the earth and all it represents.

It is also an acknowledgment of our finitude and mortality. One of the reasons why I prefer burial to Western-style cremation is that the body is lowered down into the earth and truly buried, and I find the words "earth to earth, ashes to ashes, dust to dust" a salutary and glad reminder of who and what we are. I have no theological objection to the burning of bodies, but what I dislike is the artificial and technological way in which it is done, with the pressing of buttons and the mechanistic moving or lowering of the coffin in the expensive and hygienic manner which protects us from confrontation with the reality of death and its naturalness.

I have used the word *humus*, which is a gardening, agricultural word. Our word *humility* derives from it, and the earthy color of the Franciscan habit (originally gray or ashen) is a reminder that we should be an earthy and humble people. My favorite story of Ramon Lull, the thirteenth-century Franciscan, highlights Franciscan humility.

When he was in his late seventies, not long before his martyrdom, he visited the University of Paris. He had once been revered there, but now had been forgotten, for a new scholar had appeared, the young Franciscan Duns Scotus, who had left throngs of admirers at Ox-

*ford and was now commanding attention lecturing in
philosophy at the Sorbonne.*

*One day, Ramon Lull, white-bearded and attentive,
listened to the young lecturer, nodding or shaking his
head during the lecture. Duns Scotus thought him to
be a presumptuous and ignorant old man, and turned
upon him rudely, asking what he intended as a gram-
matical question:*

> *Dominus, quae pars?*
> *(Dominus, what part [of speech] is that?)*

Ramon gently and in humility answered:

> *Dominus non est pars, sed totum.*
> *(Dominus [the Lord] is no part, but the whole.)*

We are not told how Duns Scotus reacted, but we do know
that Ramon Lull is known as the "Fool of Love," and that
he was stoned to death by the Muslims for his witness to
Christ. He was among those who thought of such a death as
an entrance into eternal life.

One of the things that Saint Francis has in common with
the Buddhist and Hindu traditions is the understanding of
death not simply as an enemy (as it is in some respects), but
as friend and sister. Such a realization is a revolutionary
discovery to many people who have long lived in the fear of
death. If I can become friendly with my own death I shall
have gained a new impetus to live, and a new serenity to
share with those around me. Everyone over thirty years of
age thinks of his or her own death; and how good it is to be
able to participate in a meditation devoted to the theme of
one's own death.

When the chestnut tree outside my window has borne its foliage, its blossom and its fruit, then the autumn wind blows through its branches, scattering thousands of chestnuts onto the grass below. As autumn gives way to winter, the sap falls, the tree loses all its leaves and it stands stark and bare. But there is no need to fear, for in the process of time, spring will come again.

I commend such thinking to you during your days of retreat, for it is an opportune time to reflect upon the transitory nature of our life on earth. Because we belong to the earth we are mortal, and affirming and embracing our mortality in a positive way can only enhance our human lives and give us the necessary humility by which we are to live.

There is also another reason. We may suddenly be faced with a diagnosis or an accident that may confront us with our imminent death, or with the kind of surgery that will reduce our mentality or mobility. This, too, we must reflect upon. I am currently reading Morris West's novel *Lazarus*. In it, the future Pope Leo XIV is threatened with death and needs radical cardiac surgery. In a perceptive and powerful interview with his Jewish surgeon Salviati, he is told of the necessary surgery and prognosis and given counsel about his attitude. The whole interview is excellent reading for a retreatant, and the following paragraph points up the mortal frailty of our human condition:

> *You will be unconscious for at least forty-eight hours, perfused with potent anaesthetics. You will continue to be fed opiates and analgesics until the discomforts are within tolerable limits. However, you will suffer something else: a psychic trauma, a personality change*

*whose dimensions still elude full explanation. You will
be emotionally fragile—as prone to tears as to rage.
You will be subject to depressions, sudden, black and
sometimes suicidal. At one moment you will be as dependent as a child, seeking reassurance after a night-
mare. The next you will be angry and frustrated by
your own impotence. Your short-term memory may be
defective. Your tolerance of emotional stress will be
greatly reduced. You will be strongly advised by the
counselors who will be working with you not to make
any important decisions, emotional, intellectual or ad-
ministrative, for at least three months...Most of these
sequelae will pass. Some will remain, diminished but
always present in your psychic life. The better your
physical condition the less will be your emotional
handicap. So, after the first period of convalescence,
you will be put on a rigid diet to lose fifteen or twenty
pounds. You will be required to do daily exercise on a
graduated scale. And if you fail to do either of those
things your psychic handicap will continue and your
physical condition will deteriorate rapidly. In short,
the whole exercise will be a painful futility. I'm sorry
to make such a huge mouthful of this, but it is absolutely necessary that you understand it. Believe me, I
do not exaggerate.*

The whole book is a perceptive unpackaging of our finitude and fallibility, well illustrating this morning's theme of
our earthiness with its attendant glory and pain.

There are other ways in which our meditation on the earth
could have taken us. We may have considered the fact that

we live in *one* world, with its diversification into nations, colors, languages, cultures, and traditions, not to speak of world religions. But all these universal questions of value, justice, equality, human need, and responsibility come down to the personal questions of love, integrity, honesty and the humility to face our own mortality.

The Hebrew text of Genesis 1:2 says that the earth, at its creation, was *tohu wa bohu*—formless and empty, with darkness over the face of the deep. Then the text goes on to say that the Spirit of God moved over the face of the waters— and so began the stirrings of life within the womb of the earth.

Exercise

In this exercise this morning I walk out to a place which affords a broad view of field, meadow, hill, or valley. Removing my shoes, I take a measured step and feel the texture of the ground beneath my feet. I become aware of the morning temperature, note the sights and sounds around me and notice the plants, trees, flowers along my way. When I get to the chosen spot I find a place to sit and observe the panoramic view around me—above or below.

Since the *earth* is my theme, I allow gratitude to arise within me for the verdant pasture and landscape. I sense my own appreciation for the variety of growth—for grass, trees, plants, vegetables, and flowers—for wild and cultivated nature.

As I reflect upon the miracle of plowing and sowing, of reaping and harvesting, I offer thanks for that process within my own life. I remember the good seeds planted by my parents when I was a child and their love which nurtured each tender plant.

Reflection upon mother earth stirs up profound feelings of warmth and embrace experienced through my earthly mother. Perhaps you may have also to deal with negative emotions here and allow forgiveness to be part of your pattern.

Motherhood of the earth also causes me to reflect upon Mary, the Mother of Jesus, as I see in my mind's eye the icon of Our Lady of Vladimir, with its compassion in Mary's eyes, the intimate closeness of Jesus the child and his mother, and the enfolding embrace and protection of her hands around the baby.

I agree with the Orthodox tradition that Jesus must be central, and Mary must not stand in his way—otherwise it becomes "Mariolatry." It is because I love "Jesus only," as Savior and Lord, that I feel an immense love and gratitude for his mother. Through her loving obedience and humility, God became incarnate for sinners, and as Scripture says, all nations will call her blessed.

So to complete the circle of meditation upon mother earth, human mortality and maternal love I turn to a poem by G. A. Studdart Kennedy. It is entitled "Good Friday Falls on Lady Day." The occasion was that one of the liturgical celebrations for Mary, Mother of Jesus, was set aside to remember Jesus' Passion and death for our redemption on Good Friday.

And has Our Lady lost her place?
Does her white star burn dim?
No, she has lowly veiled her face
Because of Him.

Men give to her the jeweled crown,
And robe with broidered rim;
But fain is she to cast them down
Because of Him.

She claims no crown from Christ apart,
Who gave God life and limb,
She only claims a broken heart
Because of Him.

Meal Preparation for

DAY 1

Fruit and Nut Risotto

4 Tbsps oil
8 ozs brown rice
2 onions, chopped
1 large sweet green pepper, chopped
4 ozs cashew nuts
8 ozs mushrooms, sliced
4 sticks of celery, chopped
4 large tomatoes (or 1 equivalent can)
2 ozs raisins
parsley, chopped
salt and pepper

Heat half the oil in a large pan. Fry the rice for several minutes, then cover with boiling water and simmer for 45 minutes (could be less time, keep checking). Drain. Heat the rest of the oil in a deep pan. Cook the onions; add the green pepper, nuts, mushrooms, and celery, and cook until soft. Add the cooked rice, tomatoes, and raisins. Season, then sprinkle with parsley.

Evening of Day 1: The Seasons

This morning we reflected upon the earth as mother, as the cradle of our mortal life from birth, through life, to death: "Dust you are, and to dust you shall return." There is a sense of rootedness and security in all that.

This evening we turn to thoughts of diversity and change within the basic stability of life on earth, illustrated by the changing seasons and the variation of weather and mood in nature. We need, therefore, to center down into an interior stillness, so that the roots of our being are anchored within the love of God. Only thus shall we experience and embrace positively the changes and chances of our fleeting world within the unity and immutability of God.

Prayer

Lord of the elements and changing seasons, keep me in the hollow of your hand. When I am tossed to and fro with the winds of adversity and the blasts of sickness and misunderstanding, still my racing heart, quiet my troubled mind.

Bring me at last through the storms and tribulations of this mortal life into the calm evening of your unchanging love; and grant that in the midst of my present perplexities and confusion I may experience your peace which passes human understanding. Through Jesus Christ, our Lord. Amen.

Scripture Passage

Read the following Scripture passages slowly: Psalm 65:
9–13 and Mark 4:35–41.

Meditation

The changing of the seasons makes for both stability and
change. There is immense delight in the diversity experienced in the variation of the seasons, for they are grounded
in the unity of the year and the fecundity of the earth. If I
say "Change and decay in all around I see," I can counter it
with "O you who change not, abide with me." As the year
rolls around and one season gives way to another, I count
the seasons of my life, and for every variation in the world
outside me I feel and experience an answering reverbera-
tion in my heart.

In the springtime there is a warming of the earth, a melting of the ice, a flowing of the waters. Living creatures asleep
or abroad during winter's death begin to breathe the warmer
air again, and my heart lifts in hope and love. After a long
winter of icy rain and battering storms on the Lleyn Penin-
sula in Wales, the gorse or furze bushes put out prolific
growth of golden yellow flowers, and the yellowhammer
builds its nest within its prickly fortress. All around in earth
and sky new life calls. Deep within the swollen waters of
sea and river the year is renewed. Springtime in my heart
indicates the turning of my life toward God, the melting of
the icy winter of sin and the springing forth of the fountain
of love.

Summertime around the monastery begins with the

spring-sown crops pushing upward. Barley and corn grow lime-green as spring freshness gives way to leafy, hot summer days, and the evening shadows bring bats twisting and turning in the evening twilight. I feel thunder heavy in the air, rejoice in the refreshing showers of rain and watch the progress of the year in the yellowing of the corn. Summer in my heart is a time of diligent labor, working at loving relationships and exploring avenues of service for God. It is a time of thirst and drought, with the accompanying need for turning aside with Christ in prayer and retreat.

These are the days of the fullness of one's energy—a time of communicating the gospel and sustaining others in the faith. The burden and heat of the day often dries up one's spiritual resources, and the danger of *accidie* and spiritual dryness is only remedied by retreat, solitude, and quiet sharing with a soul-friend and spiritual guide. Fellowship with God's people, hearing his word and receiving the sacrament of his body and blood—these things are indispensable to a mature Christian life, and this is the time to grow in knowledge and wisdom.

As summer gives way to autumn the corn and wheat turn to yellowing bronze and brown, and bright red poppies dance in the breeze and the whole earth yields its diverse fruitfulness. Our reading from Psalm 65:9–13 is a song of fruitful joy, not only from the fields of harvest, but from the field of the human heart. Fruitfulness and melancholy join hands in autumn, and there is a constant reminder in the world of nature of the fact that "we blossom and flourish like leaves on the tree, we wither and perish, but naught changes thee." Beautiful autumn mists linger in the mornings, and blackberries, sloes, and elderberries ripen in hedges. Green and yellow give way to all the riotous tints of autumn, and the lazy, drowsy humming of the bumble bee reminds us of the nectar to be found deep within the autumn flowers. This is the time for reflection upon one's life, the bringing together of all the disparate parts of a busy existence, and the cultivation of a rich interior life of prayer, storing the nectar in order that its sweetness may be spread around in love and grace.

October has been said to possess the alchemy of the seasons, and certainly it is heavy with autumn's fruitfulness in its beginning, and ending with torrential rain and clouds which blow across the grayness of the sky.

Now as November heralds the beginning of winter, my Spanish chestnut tree gives up its weight of sweet nuts. The yellow and bronze foliage of October and November fades to ocher and the withered leaves fall with the prickly chestnut cases. This tree, introduced into Britain by the Romans two thousand years ago, especially reminds me of time and eternity, for it can grow up to one hundred and twenty feet in height and may live for five hundred years. The low November sun casts dark shadows, but illuminates the ascending branches as the tree begins its winter rest.

The long nights and brief days of winter cause us to reflect upon the dying of things. But silver, gold, scarlet, bronze, and purple flash out from briar and bramble, and already the promise of new life stirs within the earth. It is no accident that the Incarnation of God among his people for their redemption is celebrated in the bleak midwinter of the year—as the Resurrection of the incarnate and crucified Lord is celebrated in the spring. There is a divine correlation between the Spirit of God indwelling the natural order and the same Spirit at work in the reconciling gospel of redemption.

Most of these reflections upon the changing seasons seem to apply only to the country-dweller or to those who visit and watch the procession of the seasons outside the concrete jungle of the city. But all of us are now immensely aware of the need to return to the soil, to protect our environment, to avail ourselves of the healing properties of the country.

All such reflection also affirms the diversity within the unity of the year, and all the maturing changes of mood and season in nature are reflected within our own souls. We are *microsomos* within the great *cosmos*, little worlds within the immensity of our planet. Such change and variation teaches us to be versatile, no less in the winter of our lives than in the spring. We have all experienced the intransigence of some young people who are averse to flexibility of thought and mood, even though they are capable of physical agility. And we have also experienced the wisdom of some old people who, though having lost the physical agility of their youth, are yet supple in mind and spirit and sensitive to the new springs of life bubbling up within them.

The old philosophers, speaking of the basic elements of fire, water, earth, and air, debated unity and diversity; and Heraclitus said that one can never step twice into the same river. There is constant change and flux in all things, and nothing ever remains the same. Therefore, as creatures of the earth, dependent upon its resources and rooted into its basic elements, we also are in constant flux. Versatility, adaptability, and flexibility are not simply virtues, but necessities which we must develop and sustain.

Both the child Jesus and old Simeon in the Temple grew in wisdom, stature, discernment, and awareness by the grace and power of the Holy Spirit. If we will respond each moment to the creative power of the same Spirit, we shall be able to adapt spontaneously to the changing seasons of our lives. If we are born of the Spirit, live in the Spirit, walk in the Spirit, and are anointed by the Spirit, then we shall develop a spiritual life which is pliable in the hands of God, flexible in our relationships with fellow creatures, but which cannot be bent to the will of violent and worldly men.

Exercise

This evening, after centering down, use a living plant or flower to symbolize the life of the Spirit in the natural world. Take some time in reflecting back to your childhood and ask yourself if you have responded positively to the "changes and chances" which have surrounded you since those days.

See if there have been any particular points of resistance, any blocks in the evolution of an easy and yielding adaptability to changes at home, at school, at work, and especially within yourself.

Ask yourself about your present situation and relationships, particularly with those you love, your spouse, your family, and those with whom you come into daily contact. See if there are ways in which you check and quench God's Holy Spirit within you, and seek ways to become more pliable in his hands. Think of yourself as malleable clay in the hands of the potter and reflect upon this prayer, perhaps repeating or singing it quietly:

Have your own way, Lord, have your own way,
You are the Potter, I am the clay;
Mold me and make me after your will,
As I am waiting, yielded and still.

Now, can you come to one or two simple conclusions as a result of this exercise, and make one or two basic decisions about your attitude toward yourself, toward your loved ones, toward your neighbors, and toward God? Don't be too ambitious, but keep mind and heart together as you seek to be more open and loving, closer to your own image of honesty and integrity.

As you go to sleep tonight, let this prayer be on your lips and in your heart:

O Lord, support us all the day long of this troublesome life, until the shades lengthen, and the evening comes, and the busy world is hushed, the fever of life is over, and our work is done. Then, Lord, in your mercy grant us safe lodging, a holy rest, and peace at the last; through Jesus Christ our Lord. Amen.

DAY 2

Sun and Moon

Morning of Day 2: The Sun

Franco Zeffirelli's film *Brother Sun and Sister Moon* portrays Saint Francis of Assisi is the sun shining in its strength and Saint Clare is the moon serenely reflecting the clear light of Francis.

The reality was not quite as romantic as the film makes out, but the analogy does hold. Francis certainly was the sun of inspiration, under God, for the renewal of the Gospel life in the midst of a decaying and corrupt Church, and Clare certainly embodied the pure light of prayer in the midst of worldliness and materialism. These great luminaries in the heavens do mediate to us the light of God's revelation and love in our dark world.

Prayer

God our Father: Your dear Son is the Sun of Righteousness, and his life-giving beams shine throughout the world. Illuminate today the dark places in my heart; chase away the gloom of doubt and depression and irradiate my whole being with the outshining of your glory. Through Jesus Christ, our Lord. Amen.

Scripture Reading

Read the following Scripture passages slowly: Genesis 1:14–19; Mark 1:32–35.

Meditation

Saint Paul understood how the world of nature illustrates the truth of the Gospel when he wrote: "God, who commanded the light to shine out of darkness, has shone in our hearts to give the light of the knowledge of the glory of God in the face of Jesus Christ" (2 Cor 4:6). The prophecy of Malachi finds its radiant fulfillment in Christ the Sun: "For you who fear my name, the Sun of Righteousness shall rise, with healing in his wings" (Mal 4:2).

One memorable experience for me happened during a symposium held at Saint David's in Wales. Early each morning there was a celebration of the Eucharist in the chapel behind the high altar of the cathedral, using Orthodox, Roman, and Anglican rites, reflecting the traditions of the Christians gathered there. One morning, we were all gathered around the altar in worship. The sun was pouring in through the clear glass of one of the great windows and we were singing a great Wesley hymn which united us in love and faith: *Christ, Whose Glory Fills the Skies.*

It was an experience like the one which the Russian messengers brought back from their exploratory visit to the Church of St. Sophia in Constantinople, when they reported of the Orthodox Mass: "We didn't know whether we were in heaven or on earth."

That St. David's experience, in such an ecumenical setting, enabled me to see Christ as the universal Sun, not limited to our religious parties or groupings.

The sun is the central body of our solar system, around which the planets revolve in their orbits and from which their light and heat is derived. It lies about ninety-two million miles from the earth—but it shines on me! Its glory is universal but its splendor is all mine! I can, if I choose, stay within my darkened house with windows blackened or curtains drawn—that is my choice. But the sun keeps on shining.

There are times, it is true, when menacing clouds and wintry skies obscure the sun's warm rays, but on those days I believe that the sun continues to shine beyond the clouds, and in its own good time will warm me again. My concern should be that I do not allow any cloud of my own making to obscure its clear light. In John Keble's words:

Sun of my soul, thou Savior dear,
It is not night if thou be near:
O may no earth-born cloud arise
To hide thee from thy servant's eyes.

There is such a thing as sun-deprivation, and I know some people whose heaviness and depression are accentuated during the months of winter, for it is increasingly recognized that part of the treatment for such a condition is sun or light therapy.

From what I remember, the ultraviolet rays of the sun activate the ergosterol in the skin, which becomes vitamin D, thus promoting general well-being as well as particular benefit to the circulatory and skeletal systems. Contemporary research has revealed definite psychosomatic changes as a result of light therapy, and I have no doubt of its objective value.

If the sun is cosmic or universal and we are microsomic, or little worlds, then if I translate these findings into the spiritual dimension it means that exposure to the Sun of Righteousness will enlighten, irradiate, and illumine all the dark places in our souls and fill us with glory.

But what about the dangers? They are twofold. First, there is the man who prefers his darkness and will not come o the light because his deeds are evil (Jn 3:19–21). He is like the sick man who does not want to be healthy because he prefers his sickness, for health involves responsibility. There are people who do not want to be exposed to the light of Christ because their lives will have to change. There are Christians like that, too. There are violent, selfish, exclusivist, pharisaic, Christians who use the clouds of religion to shield them from the Sun of Righteousness. Perhaps we are among them?

The remedy is to move out of the darkness and into the light. The method is the other way round—to allow the light to shine into the dark places; and painful though it may be, like the sun upon weak eyes, the result will be joy and glory.

But there is a second danger. The sun is dangerous. It is not simply a heavenly luminary that shines beneficently on our cold and icy world, but the blazing sun of the desert, burning and scorching because of its very nature. So God is dangerous, and we cannot gaze upon his blinding glory without shielding our poor eyes. We must *learn* to bear his glory, to gaze into his dazzling light. As William Blake says:

> *Look on the rising sun: there God does live,*
> *And gives his light, and gives his heat away*
> *And flowers and trees and beasts and man receive*
> *   Comfort in morning, joy in the noon day.*
>
> *And we are put on earth a little space,*
> *   That we may learn to bear the beams of love....*

Too much exposure to the sun's rays too quickly or in excess may cause all manner of skin diseases, for our bodies, especially in our part of the world, are not used to such exposure. Glory can burn, and the beams of love can shrivel a selfish soul. At the end of John Henry Newman's *The Dream of Gerontius*, beautifully set to music by Edward Elgar, Gerontius asks his guardian angel: "Shall I *see* my Lord?" and the angel answers that he cannot understand what he asks. The unveiled glory of God's unutterable splendor will smite and burn, will pierce and wound, will slay with its glorious beauty.

Gerontius' double exposure to the divine Love, to the "awful glance" of God will smite Gerontius beyond anything he has known in life on earth. He will be consumed and quickened by this glimpse of glory. In this moment he has realized as never before his total unworthiness, his finitude, the chasm of creatureliness which causes him to cover his eyes, and to cry from the lowest depths. It is a moment of supreme pain and supreme joy. But now he knows. Now he is aware of all the implications of all his questions, and he feels the sorrow and the joy which penetrate his being, for he longs for God.

Gazing upon the glory of the Sun of Righteousness can begin on earth, and the mystical tradition in the Church, following the biblical tradition, speaks of the twofold agony of those whose yearning for God impels them to seek him. There is the pain of shame and self-loathing because of selfishness and unlikeness—the sin shriveling before absolute holiness—and there is the immortal longing in the creature to behold the splendor and wonder of the divine Beauty. This provokes an intensity of yearning to be transformed into his likeness and beauty that is an agony to the loving soul.

We began this meditation with Saint Francis of Assisi and now we return to him. He has been called the saint who lived closest to Christ outside the New Testament, and in *The Dream of Gerontius* the guardian angel speaks of him as one of the few who, in this life, have gazed upon the glory of the crucified Jesus, the Sun of blazing glory, receiving in his body the marks of the stigmata:

There was a mortal, who is now above
In the mid glory: he, when near to die
Was given communion with the Crucified—
Such, that the Master's very wounds were stamped
Upon his flesh; and, from the agony
Which thrilled through body and soul
    in that embrace,
Learn that the flame of the Everlasting Love
Doth burn ere it transform.

The Sun is gently beneficent, imparting light and warmth, growth and fertility, illumination and glory. The Sun is dangerous, threatening those who live in darkness with dazzling, blinding glory—not because it wills to destroy but because of its very nature. If we are to bear the beams of such love, we must learn gently, but progressively, so that we shall more and more be exposed to his glory, and reflect his radiance in this dark world.

Exercise

It would be a wonderful experience to greet the sunrise during this week of retreat. Get up before dawn and hope to see and participate in the rising of the sun—and allow Jesus to rise anew in your heart. Make Charles Wesley's hymn the subject of your meditation and carry its radiance with you through the day:

Christ, whose glory fills the skies,
  Christ, the true, the only Light,
Sun of Righteousness, arise,
  Triumph o'er the shades of night;
Dayspring from on high, be near;
Daystar in my heart appear.

Dark and cheerless is the morn
  Unaccompanied by thee;
Joyless is the day's return,
Till thy mercy's beams I see;
Till they inward light impart,
Glad my eyes, and warm my heart.

Visit then this soul of mine,
  Pierce the gloom of sin and grief;
Fill me, Radiancy Divine,
  Scatter all my unbelief;
More and more thyself display,
Shining to the perfect day.

Let this radiance shine within you until evening, and then remember the ministry of Jesus as the evening sun went down as recorded in Mark 1:32–34.

The sun cannot help shining, and Jesus cannot help but stretch out his hands of compassion and healing in the light of the evening sun. If the shining of this sun is his radiance, then it will stimulate loving compassion and service in your life, and the darkness in the lives of others will be dispelled. And they will come to love him, too!

Meal Preparation for

DAY 2

Vegetable Pie

1 1/2 lbs potatoes, cooked and mashed
5 ozs brown lentils
5 ozs green lentils
1 pint stock—made by adding 2 bouillon
      cubes to boiling water
1 onion, chopped
1 sweet green pepper, chopped
a few mushrooms, sliced
2 carrots, finely sliced
2 tomatoes, chopped
2 sticks of celery, finely sliced
1/2 tsp each: mixed herbs, chopped parsley
1 clove of garlic, crushed
1 oz margarine for frying
4 ozs grated cheese (your favorite)
a little milk for the mashed potatoes

Fry onions and other vegetables, covered in a pan, until soft. Simmer lentils in the stock until tender. Mix the vegetables and the cooked lentils together. Season to taste; add the herbs and garlic. Sprinkle with grated cheese, brown under the grill. Serve with mashed potatoes.

Evening of Day 2: The Moon

The astronomer will give a quite different account of the moon and the night sky than the poet. He will say that the moon is a satellite of the earth, revolving around the earth every lunar month, being some 238,000 miles distant and having a lunar attractive force upon the tides.

The astrophysicist and astronaut will join him and share a great deal more fascinating information since humanity's landing on the moon's surface. But when we have sifted and digested all that information, there remains a whole dimension belonging to the poet, the musician, the artist, and the philosopher—not to speak of the psychologist and the theologian.

Without prejudice to the scientific attitude (for that is a gift of God also), we shall reflect more along the lines of the latter group, using the intuitive and spiritual perception which is a precious gift of our humanity.

Prayer

Heavenly Father: You have set sun, moon, and stars in their places and the music of the spheres sings your praise. As I reflect upon their glory and your handiwork, grant me a greater awareness of the wonder of your being and a deeper appreciation of your tender love. Through Jesus Christ, our Lord. Amen.

Scripture Reading

Read the following Scripture passages slowly: Psalm 8; Genesis 37:1–11.

Meditation

It is possible to turn from a scientific and objective evaluation of our world into a poetic flight of fancy and sentimental subjectivism. Such an attitude is irresponsible and not worthy of the person who would take seriously the tasks and problems before us today.

Back in my student days, studying in Switzerland, I lived in a student complex on Lake Zurich where one of the office staff had her eye on one of the Finnish students. She stood one evening where he could see her and began to sing quietly: "Blue moon, you saw me standing alone, / Without a dream in my heart, / Without a love of my own."

That's the "moony" attitude I am deploring, though I liked both B (the singer) and J (the fellow). And it worked, because they eventually married!

People in love have always lingered beneath the moon, and in times of separation have made covenants to think of each other under the same moon at a prearranged time. I can think of half a dozen "moony" romantic songs off the top of my head—and there's no harm in that. But the kind of reflection which will be productive for us in retreat is the contemplative attitude which the psalmist cultivates.

Many of the psalms have a twofold significance, in that they are grounded in personal and immediate experience of God in the human situation, and they are liturgically structured so that they may be chanted and sung in the worship of the temple.

The profound misery and ecstasy found in many of the psalms are the stuff of worship, praise, and lament among the people of God. We are not as uninhibited in worship as were some of the old Hebrews, for they could weep and cry and moan before God as well as chant, dance, and sing. It is an interesting point that even in charismatic groups where singing, dancing, and ecstatic utterances are acceptable, wailing and grief-stricken weeping are not! And yet, in a more restrained and Catholic tradition, a liturgical setting of the "Lamentations of Jeremiah" by Thomas Talus may provide an emotional outlet which would induce an experience of psychological and spiritual liberation in the worshiper.

Equally, the original and immediate experience of the psalmist in solitude under the night sky may communicate itself to the present-day reader in meditating upon the same phenomena under the guidance of the Spirit of God.

Psalm 8 is such a meditation, for it is a beautiful reflection upon the glory of God and the worth and dignity of the human being, in the context of the created order, and especially under the night sky:

> *When I look at your heavens, the work*
>   *of your fingers,*
> *the moon and the stars that you have established;*
> *what are human beings that you are mindful*
>   *of them,*
> *mortals that you care for them?*

The psalmist's reflection upon the created order, and especially the pale beauty of the moon and stars in the canopy of space, gives rise to praise and wonder.

There are people who feel dwarfed and frightened by the immensities of space, and the effect of philosophical or astronomical reflection confirms to them their own insignificance, creatureliness, and meaninglessness in so immense a cosmos. What on earth is the significance of our poor planet among the untold galaxies of the universe? How can there possibly be any meaning or purpose attached to the chance appearance of humankind, lost in the infinite stretches of solar space?

But this is not the reasoning of the psalmist, nor is it the response of the believer who considers the panorama of dazzling beauty in the night sky on a clear night under a full moon. The reason for the psalmist's faith and optimism is that he has already had experience of God, not only as creator but as redeemer. There had been times of darkness, sin, failure, and pain when he cried to the Lord from the depths, sinking in the mire of frustration and anxiety. His experience in such situations was that there is a redeeming God whose loving heart is moved with compassion toward his creation. And that saving, living, healing, forgiving, and liberating experience is a manifestation of the power that moves the sun, moon, and stars in their courses, and acts for good in a personal and intimate way in his own small life.

This, of course, involves an act or leap of faith, for there is never a time when the believer is able to demonstrate with proofs beyond doubt that there is a loving and gracious redeemer within and behind the created order.

But now let us move from the book of Psalms to a particular story in the book of Genesis, which records the dilemma and adventure of what it means to be human. The Joseph cycle of stories tells of hidden, providential care in the face of tragedy and catastrophe. It certainly needed the eye of faith and a heart of trust for Joseph to believe that there was any loving, providential God moving in or behind his life.

He was betrayed by his brothers, thrown into a pit, sold into slavery, cast aside by a jealous woman, and cast into prison. And all this in a strange land, separated from his father and alienated from his own people. But because he had an early experience of God in the depths of his soul, he could draw on the reservoir of spiritual experience and keep in touch meditatively while sinking in the mire and the rough handling of brothers or enemies.

We can locate such early childhood trust in the pastoral scene of his boyhood. He was a child who developed a contemplative faith and trust in God. His dreams were of the harvest field and the fruits of the earth. His visions were stimulated by meditation under the night sky. Sun, moon, and stars all yielded up their symbolic meaning as a guide to his own life.

Is it possible that, sitting in a cornfield under the night sky, with the serene light of the moon filling his vision, he could feel the Spirit of God speaking within the depths of his young heart? The book of Genesis says so!

The reason why this particular story appealed to me as a twelve- and thirteen-year-old boy was that I also dreamed along the coastline, meditated under the night sky, and gazed upon the face of the moon with all its serene mystery and sublime beauty. I understood something of the feeling that Joseph must have experienced because the sense of childhood wonder had never been crushed in me, and my childhood upbringing did not educate me out of that contemplative mood, which is native to the uncorrupted child.

I knew what Joseph knew because the same phenomena

faced me and the same Spirit indwelt me, and Joseph's story communicated itself and served as a pattern for my own life. This has continued over the years from the early vision of childhood, through heights and depths, in the dark places of the soul and in my evolving pilgrimage of joy and sorrow.

From my window at Glasshampton, I have seen that the moon has been waxing and waning and looked over the half-harvested cornfields from my high window. The solitary beauty of the landscape under the serene light of the moon has been breathtaking in its beauty, and has stimulated such yearning for God within my own heart, causing me sometimes to cry out for the love which lies at the heart of the changing seasons and within the world's melancholy beauty. I say "melancholy" because such a harvest scene under the light of the moon stirs up in me the memory of things I cannot express:

> *It is the melody of all sweet music,*
> *In all fair forms it is the hidden grace;*
> *In all I love a something that escapes me,*
> *Flies my pursuit and ever veils its face.*
> *I see it in the woodland's summer beauty,*
> *I hear it in the breathing of the air;*
> *I stretch my hands to feel for it, and grasp it,*
> *But oh! too well I know, it is not there.*

The contemplative who wrote those words would understand completely what I mean, and so perhaps would Joseph's father Jacob, who when listening to the account of Joseph's dreams of the night sky, kept these things and pondered them in his heart.

Another night at Glasshampton, I stepped into the central courtyard when all the house was hushed, and looked into the night sky. I was made breathless by the pale beauty of a full moon ringed around with three or four circles of misty beauty, and I realized that this is what Henry Vaughan must have looked upon when he wrote:

> *I saw Eternity the other night*
> *Like a great ring of pure and endless light,*
> *All calm, as it was bright,*
> *And round beneath it, Time in hours, days, years,*
> *Driven by the spheres...*

Space, time, and memory; prayer, thought, and wonder; worship, praise, and upsurge of love. All these under the night sky, when the world is covered in moon and shadow, under the canopy of space.

Exercise

For tonight's exercise you will need the night sky (maybe a flashlight), the Scripture passages listed on page 68, and a contemplative attitude. During the day, familiarize yourself with the Joseph story found in Chapters 37 and 47 of Genesis.

Then when darkness falls, in a spirit of mindfulness, walk out to an appointed spot where you are able to sit, allowing the story of Joseph's boyhood dreams to direct your mind to the providential guidance of God in your own life—remembering that Joseph often had to affirm by faith that which was not obvious to his senses or circumstances!

If you are fortunate enough to have a dry night and the light of the moon above you, look upon its face and say the words of Psalm 8, giving thanks for the dignity and worth that God has conferred upon the human family.

As a result of all this, you may find your curiosity stimulated to read up on the night sky. There are many basic introductions to astronomy available, and such a study after your retreat may widen the horizons of your mind and heart. And let that take you where it will—for all of it is God's world.

After half an hour or so of meditation, return mindfully to your bed, and before you go to sleep read over Psalm 148 and praise God for his creation.

DAY 3

Sea and River

Morning of Day 3: The Sea

The sea is a powerful image. It fascinates and draws to itself those who feel a deep affinity to it, and casts a strange spell of immensity and wonder (not without fear) over others who contemplate its profound mystery. It is a joyous and exulting friend but a dangerous and implacable enemy. Like God!

Those who feel sea-fever raging within them have immense reverence for the ever-changing sea. It will not yield its secrets, will not be controlled, is not subservient to the will of man, and is not to be trifled with.

Prayer

O God, whose love is without measure: Out of the depths of my own creatureliness and yearning I call to you. Out of your own immense depths of power and mystery you call to me. Enable me to enter into the beginnings of the secrets of your love, and let the poor stream of my life flow into the immensity of your Being. Through Jesus Christ, our Lord. Amen.

Scripture Passage

Read the following Scripture passages slowly: Exodus 14:10–31; Jonah 1; Mark 4:35–41.

Meditation

I have just returned from a few hours of exuberant and spontaneous joy—jumping, swimming, and playfully battling against the foam and crested waves of Caswell Bay. There were only a dozen or so doing the same, because the day was overcast and the water was cold before that first exhilarating plunge into its depths.

But after that there was the breathless and refreshing breasting of the waves, allowing myself to be caught up in the engulfing flood as wave after wave broke over my head and foam cascaded in great glory all around me.

Then, striking out into deeper water, as the chattering, laughing voices at the water's edge grew fainter, I was suspended between sea and sky, and felt again something of that scariness I always experience in deep water. It is the

edge of risk and excitement that threatens as well as calls—
even on a day in late August when there is only a slight
breeze along the sea's surface, and relative calm prevails.

I am basically afraid of the sea and at the same time en-
tranced by it. I have known it around the Western coast of
Wales since childhood, and many images of its calm and
savage cruelty impinge upon my mind as I reflect upon it.

I have observed it in many of its moods as a child, from
the mountain path, from many caves and inlets, and from
exposure to its scary pull as it ebbed and flowed, roared and
cascaded, behaving gently and wildly by day and night in
those childhood days long ago.

I remember its strange beauty as on night duty I observed
it through the dark hours from the second-floor verandah of
a hospital on the South Glamorgan coast, spread out before
me with the full moon reflected in its tranquil depths. I
scramble again up to that great hollow of rock at the extreme point of Worm's Head, as the wind blows in fitful
gusts and the heave and swell of the sea below evokes in me
such longings that cause me to cry out and weep for that
which I have not yet known but can only guess within the
profound depths of my own soul.

I walk again, alone, along the deserted coast two miles or
so north of St. David's. The intensity and tranquillity of that
time stirred within me hidden longings for solitude and exposed me to aspects of the mystery of God that I had hardly
known before. That day, on the Welsh coast, with the un-
canny sense of Celtic saints around me, I scrambled out of
my clothes and plunged into the sea, singing of the "bound-
less love of Jesus" as mighty as the ocean.

And then walking out one night into the darkness, finding a shelf of rock in order to sit quietly under the stars, facing the whispering, murmuring, tranquil sea, and half-saying, half-singing, those evocative words of Edward Carpenter's poem *By the Shore*:

> *All night by the shore*
> *The obscure water, the long white lines*
> *of advancing foam,*
> > *the rustle and thud, the panting sea-breaths,*
> > *the pungent sea-smell,*
> *The great slow air moving from the distant horizon,*
> > *the immense mystery of space*
> > *and the soft canopy of the clouds!*

The swooning thuds go on—the drowse of ocean goes on: The long inbreaths—the sharp outbreaths—the silence between.

> *I am a bit of the shore: the waves feed upon me,*
> > *they come pasturing over me;*
> *I am glad, O waves, that you come pasturing*
> > *over me...*

All that mystery. The mystical tradition understands the analogy of the strangeness and wildness of the sea, indicating the inscrutable strangeness and unknowability of God. One can be immersed at one moment in its ecstatic depths, rejoicing in being submerged in the wet glory of its gentle and playful embrace. And the next moment be threatened by its unknown terror, threatening a drowning death that causes one to tremble in cold fear.

The Old Testament bears witness that the Hebrews were never good sailors—that was left to the Phoenicians and others. The sea is often depicted as symbolizing the recklessness of wicked men, the conflicts and perplexities of the nations, and the wild cruelty of heathen peoples. Out of such depth arose terrible images of oppressive tyrants, and the image of the eternal kingdom was one in which there was no more sea.

But the sea belongs to God, and its glory and splendor can praise him in great and ecstatic rhythm, as some of the liturgical psalms reveal.

The great redemptive act of God in the liberation of his ancient people from the slavery of Egypt is shown as Moses, the prophet of God, stands with the whole company of the redeemed but terrified people at the edge of the threatening Red Sea with the forces of the Egyptian Pharaoh behind them.

Moses' staff is lifted, the prophetic word is spoken and the Red Sea parts at the will of its creator, giving a new dimension to the promise, "when you go through the waters I will be with you; and the floods shall not overwhelm you" (Isa 43:2).

In the story of Jonah, the sea becomes a terrible instrument in the hand of God to shake Jonah out of his complacency and exclusivism. His narrow and bigoted concept of God, as only for him and for the elect Jews, was shaken when he was faced with the universal love that was bigger than anything he could have envisaged.

The book of Jonah is about the God who is vaster than the ocean, whose love is immense in its proportions and profound in its inclusion of sinners. And whereas in other stories the seas and oceans can symbolize the dark enemies and tyrants of the heathen world, here the sea is an instrument in the hand of its creator to act in judgment against the disobedient prophet. But in God's judgment is mercy, and after the death and resurrection experience of Jonah one hopes he embraced the fullness of the divine Love. The Bible leaves his attitude open!

There are times, also, when created things can be instruments in the hands of dark powers. The story of the storm on the Sea of Galilee has a remarkable twist to it which is not clear at first reading.

The disciples, after a day of tiring ministry and teaching, heard Jesus say, "Let us go across to the other side." They embarked to cross the lake. Jesus soon went to sleep in the boat, and suddenly a great storm of wind and waves beat upon the boat and it began to fill with water rapidly and frighteningly.

As the water level rose in the boat, so fear rose in the hearts of the disciples and they called upon Jesus urgently to save them. As Mark tells the story, he describes Jesus standing up with authority and commanding the spirit of the storm with a powerful rebuke: "Silence! Be still!" The wind immediately died down, the waves were hushed, and there was a great calm.

The result was that the disciples were filled with an awe that was greater than their former fear, and they said to one another, "Who is this man? Even the wind and the waves obey him."

The point of the story is not simply that Jesus had power to still the elements, or even to bring peace and faith to his disciples, but that he had power over the underworld of evil.

The word of command which he used to rebuke the storm is the same formula by which he cast out evil spirits.

The Markan passage here and in the following stories (Mk 4:35—5:43) shows that Jesus has authority over demons, disease, and death, and has power in the lives of all humanity (demon-possessed *man; woman* with the hemorrhage; dead *child*).

The story of the storm on the Sea of Galilee in Mark's Gospel is a teaching story which portrays Jesus as the master of nature and of all the dark, elemental powers of the universe. He is the One who is able to put to rest all our conflicts and perplexities, to rescue us from the overwhelming power of death and from the ultimate evil. For he is Lord of all.

Exercise

You may be fortunate enough to spend your retreat within reach of the sea. If so, go and sit near it and allow yourself to be taken up into its movements and rhythm and sound and changing color.

But even if not, keep the text of Mark 4:35–41 before you and let yourself be carried imaginatively into the story.

Begin with the weariness of a hard day's ministry, feeling the physical tiredness that Jesus and his disciples felt, and then let the story unfold itself, involving you in the apprehension, fear, faith, and overwhelming awe at the authority of Jesus.

Then think of yourself as the boat, and of the disciples as the disparate and distracting fears and anxieties that have haunted your life and checked your ability to love and serve.

Be aware of Jesus as truly dwelling in your life but "asleep on a pillow," and awaken him to life within yourself by calling upon him and seeking his aid.

If you can stir up the gift of Christ within your own life, you will then have tapped the creative source of love and power which is your inheritance as a Christian, with the humble confidence and authority which comes with such a discovery.

In the past, or even now, the storm-waves of sin, perplexity, and confusion may seem to overwhelm you and bring you to your wits' end (Ps 107:23–32), but he who is within you is greater than all—master of wind and waves, ruler of the human heart.

Be still then, and become increasingly conscious of his life within yours, his power made perfect in your weakness. And give thanks!

> *Fierce raged the tempest o'er the deep,*
> *Watch did your anxious servants keep,*
> *But you were wrapped in guileless sleep,*
>   *Calm and still.*
>
> *"Save, Lord, we perish!" was their cry,*
> *"O save us in our agony!"*
> *Your word above the storm rose high,*
>   *"Peace, be still!"*
>
> *The wild winds hushed: the angry deep*
> *Sank, like a little child, to sleep;*
> *The sullen billows ceased to leap*
>   *At your will.*

So, when our life is clouded o'er,
And storm-winds drift us from the shore,
Say, lest we sink to rise no more,
  "Peace, be still!"

Meal Preparation for
DAY 3

Tomato Napoli

1 medium onion, chopped
1 clove of garlic, crushed
1 Tbsp of oil
1 1/2 lb fresh tomatoes, peeled and chopped
     (or 1 large can equivalent)
1 Tbsp tomato purée
1 bay leaf
1/2 tsp paprika
1/2 tsp dried basil
squeeze of lemon

Gently sauté the onion and garlic in the oil—do not brown. Add the tomatoes, tomato purée, and basil, plus seasonings. Simmer gently until reduced and thickened. The herbs can be varied to taste, or add a few chopped mushrooms. Serve with any kind of pasta, with plenty of grated cheese—preferably Parmesan.

Evening of Day 2: The River

The river is an image of tranquillity and fertility—a wonderful picture of the mature spiritual life spreading joy and fruitfulness wherever it flows. Its source is high in the mountains and its mouth opens into the sea—ever moving, ever flowing.

There is a river within the parish of Glasshampton Monastery, and where it flows into the Severn is the spot at which Francis Ridley Havergal is said to have composed a hymn which likens God's perfect peace to a river that flows ever fuller and deeper.

Prayer

Father of mercy and love: Let me be as a fruitful tree planted beside the river of your grace. Let me drink deeply of your Holy Spirit and bring forth fruit for the healing of the broken lives around me. Through Jesus Christ, our Lord. Amen.

Scripture Passage

Read each of the following Scripture passages slowly and carefully: 2 Kings 5:1–14; Ezekiel 47:1–12; and Matthew 3:13–17.

Meditation

The source of the Severn River is in the Welsh mountains, but the source of the river in the Ezekiel passage is the throne of God. From the fountain head of God's loving mercy flows the life-giving river, which brings freshness, vitality, and fertility wherever it goes.

To learn of such a river in our own days of contamination and pollution is a great joy, and to contemplate the possibility of a healing river stimulates the sources of vitality within ourselves.

I first read of this river of Ezekiel for a Scripture examination as a child, and whenever I have found my heart lifted by the sight of a flowing river it has brought this beautiful passage before my eyes:

> *O river of God, flow down on me,*
> *O river of God, flow out from me,*
> *O river of God, I cry to thee,*
> *O river of God, flow down on me.*

Naaman the Syrian, in our second reading, was not impressed with the Jordan River. When Elisha told him to dip himself in its waters for the cleansing of his leprosy, he spoke in adulation of the rivers of his home city: "Are not Abana and Pharpar, the rivers of Damascus, better than all the waters of Israel? Could I not wash in them and be clean?" And he went away in a rage. This was a test of humility and obedience as well as of faith. He was allowing his narrow nationalism as well as his status as commander of the Syrian army to get in the way of his healing.

There is a certain fear of "letting go" when one is immersed in a river. Often I have baptized people by immersion, and there is an act of trust involved because they have to give themselves over to be buried beneath the waters and to be brought up again into newness of life. It is a precious moment, both for the baptized and the baptizer when, hands clasped, the candidate stands up to the waist in water and the priest or minister puts his one hand over the clasped hands as the other grasps the collar of the baptismal garment.

The words are said after the confession of faith: "N____, I baptize you in the Name of the Father and of the Son and of the Holy Spirit…" and down the candidate goes as the water closes over the head, and up the candidate comes into newness and joy, buried with Christ and raised to life in him. I look forward to a much wider ecumenical practice of baptism by immersion, for it portrays sacramentally our identification with Christ in the mystery of his death and Resurrection in a way that is powerful, dynamic, and unique. The outward sign of an inward, spiritual grace.

That's what happened to Naaman. When once he had allowed his stubbornness and conceit to be broken down, and submitted in humility and utter need to Elisha's prophetic word, he dipped himself into the Jordan seven times, "and his flesh was restored like the flesh of a little child, and he was clean." What a river! What a cleansing! What a God!

This baptism in the Jordan River brings us to the baptism of Jesus, which was the significant moment of his identification with sinners for our redemption. In the Matthew account there is a feeling of the early Church's uneasiness about such an identification with penitent sinners.

It is quite clear in Jesus' mind that he was to stand in the sinners' place, offering to the Father that life of perfect obedience and penitence that we could not offer.

Also, in his Jordan baptism he was the recipient of such blessing that we could never have deserved. For when the

Holy Spirit descended upon him in power, and the heavenly voice spoke from the Glory, it was the Father's seal upon his Son, Jesus, as our representative. This means that if we are "in Jesus," all the blessings of his penitence and anointing are ours, too.

This symbolic river begins in Eden, but it is fouled and polluted by human sin and degradation. It is cleansed and renewed by the baptism of Jesus in the Jordan and appears in the paradise of God in the last book of the Bible, sounding very much like the prophetic river of Ezekiel, for the fruits of the tree beside the river are for the healing of the nations.

The baptism of Jesus in the Jordan River is part of the Church's Epiphany celebration. That word *epiphany* means manifestation, for God manifested his being and presence in a threefold manner at the Jordan. The Son was baptized in the river, the Spirit came upon him in power, and the Father spoke the words, which were the divine seal upon his ministry and work as Savior of the world.

The Bible does not teach the doctrine of the Holy Trinity in a dogmatic manner, clothed in the garb of Greek philosophical language, but in a vital and dynamic manifestation, as at the baptism of Jesus.

The rite of baptism is not a form of mysterious theological words to be learned by rote and a ritual to be conformed to in a mechanical manner as an introduction into the Church as an organization. Rather, it is an experienced identification with Christ, submitting oneself wholly to him in repentance and faith and going down with him into the waters of death to sin and self, and being raised again with all the power of resurrection life being manifested by the gift of the Holy Spirit. This is the new birth into the Church, the Body of Christ, which is a living organism and not just an organization.

When Jesus gave his precious sacraments to the Church, he chose in the Eucharist to make material bread and wine to be the body and blood by which we are sustained by him and healed by him, for the Eucharist is the medicine of immortality. And he chose in baptism the material element of water, so that it could be a drowning, an immersion, a dying to self, a burial and a cleansing, so that there could be a dramatic rising from that death into new life in the Spirit.

It is significant that after Jesus speaks of himself as the bread of life in the sixth chapter of John's Gospel, he goes on, in the seventh chapter, to speak of himself as the water of life, in a prophetic word which points to the period after his passion:

> *On the last day of the festival, the great day, while Jesus was standing there, he cried out, "Let anyone who is thirsty come to me, and let the one who believes in me drink. As the scripture has said, 'Out of the believer's heart shall flow rivers of living water.'" Now he said this about the Spirit, which believers in him were to receive; for as yet there was no Spirit, because Jesus was not yet glorified.*

Exercise

If there is a river or any expanse of water near your retreat place, let it be your area of meditation this evening.

Ponder upon the meaning of the river in the scripture passages given.

For Naaman, there was the need to let go of his stubborn pride and to submit himself unreservedly to the word of the prophet, and this led to his baptism of cleansing and healing.

The river in Ezekiel speaks of the baptized believer, planted by the river of fertility and bringing forth healing fruits of love and compassion.

Then reflect upon the baptism of Jesus. Spend time in thinking about the willingness of Jesus to be identified with us in our sinfulness. Not that he had sinned but that he entered willingly into the bearing and sharing of our darkness, becoming our Representative before the Father, and offering in his birth, life, death, and Resurrection that perfect life which we could not offer. And now, incorporated into him by baptism, we die and rise in newness of life to love and serve him on earth, and thereafter to reign with him in glory.

You may like to sing your gratitude and love (choose a hymn that is suitable), or anyway read the following verses by F. Pratt Green on the baptism of Jesus:

> *When Jesus came to Jordan*
>   *to be baptized by John,*
> *he did not come for pardon,*
>   *but as his Father's Son.*
> *He came to share repentance*
>   *with all who mourn their sins,*
> *to speak the vital sentence*
>   *with which good news begins.*

He came to share temptation,
*   our utmost woe and loss;*
for us and our salvation
*   to die upon the cross.*
So when the Dove descended
*   on him, the Son of Man,*
the hidden years had ended,
*   the age of grace began.*

Come, Holy Spirit, aid us
*   to keep the vows we make;*
this very day invade us,
*   and every bondage break;*
come, give our lives direction,
*   the gift we covet most—*
to share the resurrection
*   that leads to Pentecost.*

DAY 4

Mountain and Valley

Morning of Day 4: The Mountain

I sit down this morning with my Bible before me and rest in the quietness before the ascent of Mount Tabor with Jesus and the disciples. Before I read, I reflect upon the joy and privilege of this quiet time and place, and ask the Lord to help me understand what it means to ascend with him into the high places of prayer and to enable me to see him in all his glory and beauty.

Prayer

Heavenly Father, your Son was transfigured with radiant
glory on the holy mountain before he suffered death upon
the cross. Enable me to see through the suffering of this
present time to the glory that will be revealed. Transform
me into his likeness from glory to glory, in his name and by
the power of your Holy Spirit. Through Jesus Christ, our
Lord. Amen.

Scripture Reading

Read the following Scripture passage slowly: Luke 9:28–36.

Meditation

This passage carries me into the heart of Jesus' longing—to
do the Father's will. He not only knew that the cross was
before him, but he had recently warned his disciples of it at
Caesarea Philippi. And now he was ascending the mountain. He took his three closest disciples with him, and yet he
was alone. And in his loneliness was his strength, for it was
there that as man he was filled with the glory of the Father.

As he prayed, the appearance of his face, his flesh, his
garments became transfigured with light. I close my eyes
now, and gaze upon his glory:

> *Once upon a mountaintop*
> *There stood three startled men,*
> *And watched the wheels of nature stop*
> *And heaven break in.*

Their friend of every day
The face they knew for his
They saw for one half-hour the way
He always is.

And then came Moses and Elijah, bearers of law and prophecy. They share his glory and speak of his departure, his destiny, his death. The word for *departure* in the text is *exodus*, and Jesus was about to tread the wilderness of the unknown on his way to his exodus—to Calvary.

All this only confirmed to Jesus the rightness of the way— the only way he could take. The mingling of radiant glory and the darkness of the way only makes me feel more keenly the love and pain in Jesus' heart.

The three disciples had fallen asleep, and now they wake to all this transcendent glory—no wonder they were afraid! One moment they sank down into a sleep as Jesus was pray- ing—perhaps they were exhausted by the climb—and the next moment they were surrounded by a transcendent glory, which bathed the heavenly figures in the *Shekinah* of God. Peter remembered that Moses had reflected this glory when he descended from Mount Sinai with the tables of the law (Ex 34:29–35). But that glory is lost in the glory of these moments, above the brightness of the sun. Peter cried out, astonished and afraid: "Master, it is good that we are here" and he longed to busy himself in some religious activity, for beholding the glory was too much for him: "Let us build three shrines…."

Help me now, Lord, to gaze upon your glory—to see in you the fulfilment of law and prophecy—to know that Calvary-love that burns in your heart.

I understand why Jesus took his disciples up the mountain. Here, alone, I am able to see ordinary things transfigured, in ways that were not open to me in the rush and complexity of my daily life in the valley. I know I cannot remain here—but I must be here now—wholly here, for it is a place *of* vision and transformation. Was the radiant glory in Jesus or in their eyes? I think it was in both! Perhaps Peter thought of the mountain as a place of escape for Jesus. Certainly he would have Jesus evade the cross if he could. But for Jesus it was the place of vision, of confirmation of the glory that precedes the suffering.

And then the overshadowing cloud. Great fear overtook the disciples as they entered it, and how they trembled as the divine word spoke from the mystery: "This is my Beloved Son, my Chosen, listen to him." Jesus, their friend and brother, was bathed in unutterable glory. And as they gazed in wonder the patriarchs faded away, and they saw Jesus only!

The effect upon me this morning is found in the last few words of the reading: "The disciples kept silent and told no one in those days anything of what they had seen." It was not time to share, to witness, to communicate, but only to savor his loving presence, to wait in silent trembling before him, to rest in his love. He is no longer simply the compassionate friend and brother, but the mighty Savior, the Lord of all, the image of the Father's radiant glory. Blessed be his name!

Exercise

I shall try *to* walk today upon some high rise or some ascending path that leads higher. To behold Jesus upon the mountain gives me a higher understanding of his Person in the glory of the Father. Jesus, my friend and brother, is also my Savior, my Mediator, my Lord. The high mystery of God is above and beyond my understanding. I remember that description in Rudyard Kipling's *Kim*, when in his long journey with Kim, the Lama, would stretch out his hands in yearning

> *toward the high snows of the horizon. In the dawn they flared windy-red above dark blue, as Kedarnath and Badrinath, kings of that wilderness, took the first sunlight. All day long they lay like molten silver under the sun....For all their marching Kedarnath and Badrinath were not impressed: and it was only after days of travel that Kim, uplifted upon some insignificant 10,000-foot hummock, could see that a shoulder knot or horn of the two great lords had—ever so slightly—changed outline.*

In myself I find this longing and yearning as I walk and ascend today—this enveloping sense of God's mystery. But also the mystery of the swirling mists, the challenge of heights beyond my knowing, exposes my fear and trembling.

Robin Brooke-Smith shared his retreat with me last year in order to prepare himself to lead an expedition to Mount Kenya. Now he writes to me of the Kami Camp at fifteen thousand feet, dominated by huge, soaring walls of Batian and the rock faces of Point Peter and Point Dutton—a harsh world of glaciers, moraine, and rock. Excitement and anticipation filled him as the dream was about to be fulfilled, and then gave way to apprehension as doubts flooded in and dangers loomed all around. But there was no way back and the restless night ended with the 5:30 A.M. wake up. I have his letter before me and translate his words into my own spiritual fears and apprehensions:

You feel rotten at that hour, particularly at fifteen thousand feet. At that moment part of me would have willingly given up—wanted to escape from the trap of circumstance. But another part of me wanted to get on. We set off round the base of the peak to the foot of the North Face. Felt awful, puffing and panting, body protesting at such exertion at this early hour. Then came the first pitches, apprehension gives way to delight as the sun shines and the climbing goes well. We gain height. Sudden difficult bits dent one's optimism. The cloud comes in, cold sets in, tiredness returns, more doubts emerge but we continue. The climb has a momentum all its own. The mountain nudges, and goads and lures us upwards. The hard moves at about half-height are climbed, we go higher. Now we feel committed—no turning back now. The nagging verticality below eats into the consciousness. I think mountain men learn to shut out height and exposure. People often say, "I couldn't do that, I'm scared of heights." I think we are all scared of heights, only the climber learns to blot it out.

Anyway, on we go and finally in the late afternoon we arrive at our bivvy site. A perch high up in the clouds, teetering on the edge of the summit ridge. Isolation. The swooping North Face, the complex of arêtes and towers and amphitheaters becomes simplified into one single ridge leading to one single summit. One high place. One. I am occupied with simplicities. Chipping ice from cracks, melting it for water, eating, sleeping. There is exhilaration with the beauty and grandeur of the place. The cloudscape below us is breathtaking, so are the stars after dark, so many of them, so clear, so cold, so remote. All these impressions make up a fantastic world, very much "other" than our normal world—the world of the valleys and plains and business as usual, homely and comfortable. This is different.

And all the time Robin is sharing geographically what we have shared spiritually. And we are both afraid.

And so today I walk, within my own capacity, and yet ascending some incline appropriate to my surroundings, and as I walk I sing:

> *Christ, upon the mountain peak*
> *Stands alone in glory blazing.*
> *Let us, if we dare to speak,*
> *With the saints and angels praise him*
> *   —Alleluia!*
>
> *Trembling at his feet we saw*
> *Moses and Elijah speaking.*
> *All the prophets and the Law*
> *Shout through them their joyful greeting*
> *   —Alleluia!*

Swift the cloud of glory came,
God proclaiming in its thunder
Jesus as his Son by name!
Nations, cry aloud in wonder!
Alleluia!

This is God's beloved Son!
Law and prophets fade before him:
First and last, and only One,
Let Creation now adore him:
Alleluia!

Meal Preparation for

DAY 4

Vegetable Curry

1 large onion, chopped
1 large sweet green pepper, chopped *or*
    1 small cauliflower, divided into florets
1 large carrot, thinly sliced
2 Tbsps oil
1 can tomatoes *or* 1 Tbsp tomato paste
1 heaped Tbsp mild curry powder
1/2 tsp turmeric
1 clove of garlic, crushed
cornstarch for thickening
1 pint boiling water
4 ozs green or brown lentils
salt to taste

Brown onion and vegetables in the oil. Add the tomatoes or the paste. Sprinkle on the curry powder and spices, stir well; add the garlic. Sprinkle on the cornstarch, stirring all the time, and add the boiling water. Add the lentils, cover and simmer gently until they are tender. Season with salt. Serve with boiled rice, chutney, sliced raw vegetables, fried poppadums, or sliced bananas. Accompany with hard-boiled eggs.

Evening of Day 2: The Valley

From the mountain to the valley. It's more than a geographical journey, and I wonder how many mountain and valley experiences there can be? How did Moses feel when he came down from Sinai, blazing with glory, to find the idolatry and fornication of the Israelites? How did Abraham feel after the terror and relief of Mount Moriah when little Isaac was restored to him and the ram was sacrificed in his stead? And what about Elijah after he had been exposed to the noise and thunder of wind and fire about Horeb and the mighty voice of God was heard in a quiet interior whispering?

Prayer

My Father: I long for the mountain, but I live in the valley; I gaze upon your glory, but am surrounded by pain and darkness. Let the radiance of your Holy Spirit shine in my heart that people in the valley of the shadow of death may be illumined by the light of hope and salvation. Through Jesus Christ, our Lord. Amen.

Scripture Reading

Read the following Scripture passage slowly: Mark 9:14–29.

Meditation

The disciples didn't understand the meaning of the Transfiguration. That's why Jesus commanded them to silence.

More than ever now he was *Messiah* to them—but their ideas of Messiah were tied to political power, glory, might, and military strength. If they had blabbed about Moses and Elijah appearing on the mountain, about visions of light and glory, about clouds and voices from heaven, it could have stirred up the worst hopes of the disciples and the violent element of the Zealots. So Jesus emphasized his rejection, suffering and pain, and his seeming surrender to the worst the world could do. How perplexing it must have been.

My valley is sometimes like that. I've glimpsed the glory—I believe not only that there is radiance and healing and forgiveness in the heart of God, but that the divine Love is at the heart of all things—and will conquer ultimately.

But down in the valley it is difficult to communicate it— and often silence is best, especially when praying with those who this week are in my heart: the young wife whose cancer of the spine has caused her baby to be aborted—and now she is paralyzed; the growing cancer of the woman whose husband died just months ago and who herself raised so much money for cancer research; the child of three years who has a double tumor of the brain and whose family has just written to ask for prayer. Down in the valley!

When Jesus and the three came down from the mountain there was no visible evidence of the Transfiguration light upon Jesus. And the remaining disciples were despairing and impotent, having failed to help a poor epileptic boy.

The Church pictured here is portrayed too clearly for comfort. On the one hand there is Peter wanting to stay on the mountain to build religious shrines, and on the other the group of disciples, unable to help the poor epileptic child and his father, stung by the pointed criticism of the scribes, and reduced to a theological discussion of the problem they couldn't solve!

It was by his own initiative that Jesus appeared at that moment, and although he was now quite clearly on the path to the cross yet his whole attention was given to the human need down in this valley.

This is my problem. I am filled with mystical yearnings about the mountain, the mystery, the transfiguring radiance, and even the high romance of the Calvary road. But when in *this* valley the epileptic child of this troublesome father appears in my path, my impotence reveals the emptiness of my claims to the transfiguring power of Christ.

I want even the valley to be verdant and fruitful. I want to walk contemplatively in the beauty of the valley at eventide. But Jesus leads me to *this* valley. After my retreat I shall return to my own valley of service—and my version of this boy will present itself to me. I want to learn now how the transfiguring power of the mountain can help me in the valley.

I am amazed at the attitude of Jesus. He was faced with the overwhelming confirmation of the Calvary road that loomed before him. Then he walked into the situation of the complete impotence and faithlessness of the disciples who had given in to theological hair-splitting with the scribes. And the boy began writhing in epileptic convulsions before him, foaming at the mouth and helpless. In spite of all this, Jesus said, "Bring him to me!"

I'm glad he did not lay aside his compassionate love and healing power until he had dealt with the unbelief of the disciples. The child might well have died! If we waited for a faithful and obedient Church before the Lord met human need, we would wait forever!

I like to think that Peter, James, and John joined their secret faith with Jesus as he listened to the plaintive cry of the father. Jesus patiently spoke with him, drawing him out, bringing him to confession and tears. The father was so close to his dear son that he spoke in yearning for them both: "If you can do anything, have pity on us and help us."

I hear now that lovely dialogue between Jesus and the father. "If you can!" exclaims Jesus. "All things are possible to him who believes." And the father cries out (and some versions add "with tears"), "Lord, I believe; help my unbelief!"

Then strange things began to happen. There was some kind of a stirring, for people came running, Jesus began rebuking powers of darkness, and it became clear that there was more than epilepsy here. Strange convulsions shook the boy and there was a struggle and confrontation between Jesus and the dark powers.

The father seemed to understand, for his faith blazed up in spite of discouragement. He had gone beyond the impotence of the disciples in his appeal to Jesus. Although the boy was lying rigid and cold on the ground—the people said he was dead—yet the power of Jesus vibrated in the air and in the soul of the weeping father. Jesus took the boy by the hand, lifted him up, and gave him back to his father.

Down in the valley. That's where I am this evening. Perhaps with the impotent disciples or perhaps with the three who have come down from the mountain. But *here* is the source of my strength and power. I don't look to the Church but to the Savior. The Church is fallible, impotent, and sometimes busy theologizing or debating in the valley of unbelief. "Why couldn't we cast it out?" they asked Jesus. And he began to talk to them patiently and lovingly about prayer.

Exercise

The valley is a lowly place—sometimes a place of humiliation, sometimes a place of impotence. But in this text it is a place of lowly service. I walk this evening, not like this morning's walk into high places of peace and joy—but here in the quiet I make an inward journey into the low and dark places of my life.

1. I walk into my *past*. I descend into those places (or that one place) where I feel pain, guilt, and remorse. I live and feel again the hurt and grief I have caused another, and the possible or real brokenness that is the outcome. But as I walk into my past I walk with Jesus, for as the sounds of my past sin and failure cause me pain again, so he pours in his balm of forgiveness and healing.

2. I walk into my *future*. I let go of all the anxious worries and concerns that sometimes haunt me. Left to myself I could repeat all my past follies and expend my energies and hopes upon vain ambitions. But Jesus walks with me here. And as we walk together I realize that most of my fears are based upon worldly concerns. Even if they overtook me they would not be able to conquer me, for nothing on earth or in hell can separate me from the love of God in Jesus my Lord.

3. I remain in the *present* moment. The Lord Jesus is here. The past is behind—the future is not mine to see. But this present moment is mine—and his! I remember the words of the Shepherd Psalm and let them shine on me: "Yea, though I walk through the valley of the shadow of death I will fear no evil; for you are with me!" And in this valley of meditation I affirm his faithfulness.

DAY 5

Wilderness and Garden

Morning of Day 5: The Wilderness

This morning God calls me into the wilderness. It may not be for confrontation with demonic powers—that is much further along the way than I am at present. But it is certainly to be open and vulnerable before him! I realize dimly that I can only be truly alone in his presence and that my solitude is validated by the guarantee of his enfolding love. The demons may be those of my own unconscious evasions and fears. But if the solitude is "in him," then I can face it, look deep into my own soul, and then gaze into the beauty shining from his face.

Prayer

My Father: This whole week is set aside for quiet reflection, for immersion in solitude. Especially this morning, I
meditate on the solitude of Jesus in the wilderness. Even in
that lonely place there were attacks by Satan and ministry
by angels. But through it all was the awareness of your loving presence. Let that awareness be mine today. Through
Jesus Christ, our Lord. Amen.

Scripture Reading

Read the following Scripture passage slowly: Luke 4:1–13.

Meditation

Luke and Matthew say that Jesus was *led* into the desert.
Mark says that he was *driven*! But both by the Spirit! I begin to understand that. It is the work of the Holy Spirit and
of the human spirit. I am both led and driven.

This morning I acknowledge that the pattern of Jesus is
my pattern and I am here to understand how my own small
life is patterned, rooted, and grounded upon and within his.

Jesus' spirit was so saturated and suffused by the Holy
Spirit after his baptism that he was drawn inexorably into
the solitude of the desert. This encapsulates the ideas of being both led and driven by the interior indwelling Spirit of
God. The chasm between Jesus and me seems infinite, for
he was open and pliable to the Father's will. Yet the amazing thing is that I am here—I have actually responded to the
drawing power of the Holy Spirit within my own spirit and

have been brought here where other voices are silenced, and where I can be open to what is being said in the depths of my own soul.

The second thing is that Jesus was open to the voice from "the other side" and only by such exposure could he clearly see the way ahead. Only thus could he formulate the basic principles by which his life was to be lived, and only thus could the way of gentleness, hiddenness, and reconciliation be affirmed. Though Satan had no part in him and though the satanic suggestions came from "outside," yet they had to be presented *within* the reflective mind of Jesus for them to be looked at, considered, and rejected. I am not to suppose that these dark suggestions were made in any bodily form, but arose within the wilderness of Jesus' solitude. Also the process of hearing, considering, and rejecting such suggestions involves the affirmation of deeper, truer, more basic values that arose from the very depths of his soul—an affirmation of the *imago dei*, the image of God in which humanity was made. This is the context in which I consider this passage this morning.

I need, as a forgiven sinner, to affirm the image of God in which I am remade in Christ, and to listen to those deep yearnings which come from my innermost soul. Perhaps I can only know the true meaning of my own forgiveness as I learn the depths of my evasions and subtle refusal to face myself as I really am. If I do this, then I can hope that from that very ground of the soul where the Holy Spirit indwells my human spirit I will experience the transformation of being, which is the essence of true conversion.

Jesus is in the desert as the representative of our humanity, as the Second Adam. The desert is the place of testing, where Israel received the revelation of God, where God spoke to Moses from the burning bush and the Sinai mountain. The desert is the place of stripping, confrontation, purification and renewal. Here it is that Jesus' temptations evoke response and reaction in my own soul.

1. *Stones into bread*   Perhaps this is the temptation of the good being the enemy of the best. Certainly for Jesus it was the invitation not only to give people material goods but to use such power for the political manipulation of others to his will.

The temptation consisted in the abandonment of the messianic role of the Suffering Servant for the popular role of political messiah, gratifying immediate and material needs. But it was clear to Jesus that this was not his way.

I am tempted to manipulate people too, and I see that it is a form of bribery: the using of my powers of influence or communication to impose my will or convert people to my way, to bend them to my will.

Is this because of crude arrogance and pride on my part, or is it because I am really vulnerable and lacking in love, and I need constant affirmation by others because I am afraid to face myself? The wilderness is the place for such questions.

2. *The offer of power*   The second temptation for Jesus seems to be that of fulfilling people's popular expectations—the messiah who would lead a patriotic people into political freedom from the yoke of the oppressing power.

Some of the disciples held this concept of messiah, and expected Jesus to set up a new Davidic throne in Jerusalem and lead a revolution against "the Lord's enemies."

It was quite clear to Jesus that the wielding of political power involves violence, territorial aggression, and bloodshed, with the philosophy of the end justifying the means. Jesus calls Satan's bluff here, for the world as "good earth" does not belong to him and Jesus did not want the kind of political and territorial dictatorship that Satan could offer. "If my kingdom were of this world then would my servants fight," he later said to Pilate, "but my kingship is not from the world."

Every age has its worldly temptations and they seem to cluster around money, ambition, power, influence, reputation. The abuse of sexuality is quickly seized upon by the Church as temptation—and so it is—but these other sins are more deadly in Jesus' eyes.

If a Christian is called by God to work in the world of politics it is quite certain, according to Jesus' principles, that the path will be a hard and thorny one. It must be the path of justice, equality, compassion, and not a way of violence, manipulation, and the raping of the poor and of other "undeveloped" nations. One of the tenets of Buddhism is "right livelihood"—one does not engage in a work or profession that compromises or negates the profession of gentleness and compassion. It is, by such a token, a part of Christian discipleship also. I ask myself in the light of this temptation if I am able to do my job, engage in my profession, and do my daily work without harm to others.

3. *Throw yourself down*   The third temptation is that of being a sensational wonder-worker. To throw himself down the 450 feet into the Kedron Valley from a pinnacle of the

temple without being harmed would certainly have drawn a following—but at what cost?

Jesus had already made two great renunciations. He would not command power by supplying people's temporal wants. Neither would he bribe or purchase a following by the way of political power and violence. The third temptation was that of evading any real risk, of calling on angelic and divine powers to protect him, avoiding vulnerability to human suffering, pain, and darkness. Jesus would have been setting conditions and limits to the way of suffering love; but only by the complete and open risk of vulnerability could the world be redeemed.

When Jesus was arrested in the garden of Gethsemane one of his disciples tried to defend him and cut off one of the ears of the high priest's servant. Jesus touched the ear with his healing power and said:

Put your sword back into its place; for all who take the sword will perish by the sword. Do you think that I cannot appeal to my Father, and he will at once send me more than twelve legions of angels? But how then should the scriptures be fulfilled, that it must be so? (Mt 26:52–54).

Jesus knew the way he was to go, and he fully intended to take it. The temptations were not sham, they were *real*, but they *really* showed Jesus as he was—the Son who was lovingly obedient in all things to his Father. W. H. Vanstone captures the feeling in this hymn:

Love that gives, gives ever more,
gives with zeal, with eager hands,
spares not, keeps not, all outpours,
ventures all, its all expends.

Drained is love in making full,
bound in setting others free,
poor in making many rich,
weak in giving power to be.

Therefore he who shows us God
helpless hangs upon the tree;
and the nails and crown of thorns
tell of what God's love must be.

Here is God: no monarch he,
throned in easy state to reign;
here is God, whose arms of love
aching, spent, the world sustain.

Now I observe Jesus' ability to stand in time of temptation. He is able to maintain his stance because he is filled
with the Holy Spirit and because he has the word of Scripture in his heart. In his *heart*, not merely in his head.
Shakespeare's Antonio says: "The devil can cite Scripture
for his purpose." That is head-knowledge of Scripture, and
the devil can manipulate the letter of Scripture for his own
ends. Christendom is rent in schism by contradicting interpretations of Scripture, and the more exclusivist a sect
becomes the more it quotes (and often misinterprets)
Scripture.

Jesus' use of Scripture was compatible with the nature

and character of God. He affirmed that materialism and the
way of sensuality was not the road to God's kingdom; that
compromise with secular values was not the way to integrity; that exhibitionism and sensationalism was not the way
to the devotion and loyalty of men and women.

Because he was a Spirit-filled man with Scripture in his
heart, he was a man of integrity, of compassion and humility. He was willing to walk the path of suffering, darkness,
and death in order to bring healing, light, and immortality to
the world. And in doing so he confronted the powers of darkness and put them to open flight.

Temptation was not at an end. There were many more
battles to be fought, but the spiritual principles of his life
and of the kingdom were laid down and the essential victory had been won. His light blazes with glory, piercing my
darkness—and I feel its warmth and live in its radiance.

Exercise

I find three stones and lay them before me as I sit in meditation, each one representing one of the temptations, and I
label them, asking the Lord to show me how I can be or
have been guilty of succumbing to such temptations.

1. *Physical gratification*   I meditate upon my own ex-
cesses. Am I guilty of gluttony, of drunkenness, misuse of
tobacco or drugs? Do I flaunt my sexuality, trade it for affection, or do I allow my mind or body to become involved
in immoral practices? Jesus' fasting, asceticism, and chas-
tity are a clear rebuke to excessive or abusive physical gratification. Let me think positively. Do I rejoice in my physi-

cal abilities and my sexual awareness? Am I in control and do I give my body care, exercise, and proper nutrition? Is my sexual life healthy and reciprocative? Do I treat others tenderly, lovingly, and responsibly? Am I chaste? If I am celibate, do I allow my natural affection to spring up from the source of love and joy? With or without genital relationship, am I happy as a sexual human being? If not, have I someone to whom I can talk and share in complete trust and confidence? If not, ought I to do something about it?

2. *Psychological manipulation*   Do I really know what kind of a person I am? Do I project so many images of myself that I have lost my own identity—or perhaps have never known it? Do I practice any form of mental manipulation of others in my family, peer group, or job? Have I created such a public or professional image of myself that I cannot move out into the freedom of growth into maturity and change? Jesus refused the offer of the kind of power that manipulates or devalues others. Am I prepared to use psychological pressure to get my own way, and will I tread on others to achieve my own ambitions? Do I "buy" people with money, influence or the offer of power in any of its forms—and can I be bought? What is my price?

Positively, am I willing to be nonviolent psychologically as well as physically? In lifestyle, opinion, debate and argument, am I willing to engage only in open, honest, and sensitive exchanges? Can I be gentle without being sentimental and soft? And can I be firm and clear in my principles without being manipulative or repressive toward others? Can I allow disagreement or disagree with others and still live amicably with differing opinions? These are questions of maturity and integrity. If I am uneasy in facing them, am I willing to go to someone to talk the issues over?

3. *Spiritual triumphalism*   Jesus would not yield to spectacular claims to spirituality. Christians can be "proud" of their liturgy, authority, spirituality, charisms, or social awareness. These may be denominational as well as local and personal sins. We may even be proud of our humility, or our claims to charismatic gifts may smack of spiritual one-upmanship. The only valid proof of belonging to Christ is compassionate love: all else may be counterfeit or become idolatrous—whether cathedral or house church! Am I not only willing to share fellowship with my fellow-Christians, but open to learn from them in areas I don't understand? Dialogue means not only listening as well as sharing, but the willingness to change. Listen to Augustine's dictum:

> *Let me ask of my reader:*
> *Wherever, alike with myself he is certain,*
>   *there to go on with me;*
> *wherever, alike with myself he hesitates,*
>   *there to join with me in enquiring;*
> *wherever he recognizes himself to be in error,*
>   *there to return to me;*
> *wherever he recognizes me to be so,*
> *there to call me back.*

This principle of spiritual humility is not incompatible with firm principles and clear views, but it does allow me to be flexible, sensitive, and open to change where revelation and love demand it. And this principle can be translated into all parts of my life, thought, and work. Spirituality is not quoting Scripture, but living in the light of truth and love.

In my wilderness solitude can I discern devilish temptations, and am I open to the loving will of God? Only thus will I return to my daily life in the power of the Holy Spirit.

Meal Preparation for

DAY 5

Cauliflower and Onion Scramble

1 medium head cauliflower
1 Tbsp butter
1 medium onion
4 or more eggs
a little milk
salt and pepper to taste

Break the cauliflower into florets and cook in water until *al dente*—or just cooked. Melt the butter in a frying pan and gently fry the onion, sliced into rings, but without browning it. Add the cooked cauliflower pieces. Beat the eggs with the seasoning and pour, together with the milk, into the pan containing the onion and cauliflower. Stir together until the eggs are set. Serve with toast or mashed potatoes.

Evening of Day 5: The Garden

It is evening time—time for the garden of Gethsemane. Familiarity with the words of the text have dulled my appreciation and sensitivity in the past. But here tonight, in this place and alone, I feel the moving sacredness of the scene, which brings to mind a passiontide hymn:

> *Go to dark Gethsemane*
> *   You who feel the Tempter's power;*
> *Your Redeemer's conflict see,*
> *   Watch with him one bitter hour.*
> *Turn not from his griefs away,*
> *Learn of Jesus Christ to pray.*

Prayer

Heavenly Father: In the dark stillness of the garden, as the Savior prays in deep anguish of soul, and while the disciples sleep for sorrow and heaviness, let me share something of your sorrow, and feel the pulse of your compassion. My spirit is willing; let me not be overwhelmed by the weakness of my flesh. Through Jesus Christ, our Lord. Amen.

Scripture Passage

Read the following Scripture passages slowly: Mark 14:32–42; Luke 22:40–46.

Meditation

I recall that sad incident before the Gethsemane story:

> *Jesus said to them, "You will all fall away; for it is
> written, 'I will strike the shepherd, and the sheep will
> be scattered.' But after I am raised up I will go before
> you to Galilee."*
>
> *Peter said to him, "Even though they all fall away, I
> will not." And Jesus said to him, "Truly I say to you,
> this very night, before the cock crows twice, you will
> deny me three times." But he said vehemently, "If I
> must die with you I will not deny you." And they all
> said the same* (Mk 14:27–31).

How like the disciples! How like me! It was not easy for
them. There was a certain scandal in following Jesus which
culminated in the scandal of the cross. To follow him meant
sharp conflict with the forces of evil. It meant integrity in
living, ascetic penitence, basic poverty of lifestyle, and the
adoption of "faith-values." This meant trust, hope, and love
in place of money, power, houses, and lands. All this, it
seems, the disciples were willing to accept—but Jesus was
going further.

It was towards the scandal of the cross that he moved—
the yielding of his very life. And this terrified the disciples.

As they approached Gethsemane, it was clear that Jesus
also was weighed down by the intense burden of grief and
heaviness. The words that introduce the garden scene warn
us away from a superficial reading and open up the interior

pain and agony of Jesus. The words of the old version ring in my heart from my childhood reading of them:

And they came to a place which was named Gethsemane And he taketh with him Peter and James and John, and began to be sore amazed, and to be very heavy; And saith unto them: "My soul is exceeding sorrowful unto death: tarry ye here and watch" (Mk 14:32–34).

And Luke adds even more harrowing verses:

And there appeared an angel unto him from heaven, strengthening him. And being in an agony he prayed more earnestly: and his sweat was as it were great drops of blood falling down to the ground (Lk 22:43–44).

These are fearful words—that Jesus was *sore amazed, very heavy, exceeding sorrowful unto death, in an agony.* Modern translations have struggled to find words to communicate the pain and grief, the fear and terror reflected in the Greek text. This is a strange and sacred part of Scripture.

It was as if we had stumbled into the private garden where the struggle and conflict between heaven and hell was taking place. The beginnings of Jesus' wrestling with the powers of darkness are found here. It is an awesome place, and even those whom Jesus chose to be near him in his hour of utter need could not stay awake. They slept not simply through exhaustion, but because of the cold and clammy fear that surrounded them so that they could not face staying awake in Gethsemane.

The name of the garden means "oil-press," and here it was that Jesus was being crushed under the grief and burden of the world's sorrow and sin—crushed so that the oil of balm and forgiveness could be poured into the world's gaping wounds.

The fear and amazement that seemed to engulf Jesus in Gethsemane did not strike him suddenly or without warning. As they had walked together on the road to Jerusalem, Jesus told the disciples of the fate that awaited him there; of the antagonism of the secular and religious authorities who were threatened by his preaching of nonviolence, poverty, and forgiveness of one's enemies. He prophesied his arrest, imprisonment, and death. As he spoke of these dark realities, the chilling mists of fear and amazement began to close around the listening disciples, even though they did not understand the implications of his words (Mk 10:32–34).

One of the things that moves me deeply as I reflect on this text this evening is the utter loneliness of Jesus. It was not simply that Jesus faced the world with a truth or philosophy that was not acceptable, or even that he was *contra mundum*, against the world, in his attitudes and way of life. All that was true, of course. But men of such caliber and courage are able to bear their burden and communicate their vision because they have a following, a group, or at least *someone* who understands, supports, and cares. Here, in Gethsemane, the loneliness of Jesus seems absolute. Even those three…and even that *one* beloved disciple…all of them fell asleep. And within the hour, the text goes on to say, "they all forsook him and fled."

When the text portrays Jesus as "exceedingly sorrowful unto death" it brings before me two amazing truths. First, that there is the implication that Jesus' grief was so great that he could have died in Gethsemane. Perhaps that is why the Lukan text speaks of angelic ministry strengthening him so that his physical frame could bear up under the strain. There was something inexorable, inevitable, and foreordained about Calvary, which is emphasized not only in the gospel story of Jesus (Lk 24:25–27) but also in the theology of the early Church (1 Pet 1:18–20). But there is great comfort here, too. If it was the divine will that Jesus should enter into suffering and death, bearing and sharing our burden, it could only be done if Jesus openly and willingly assented to it. Also, it meant that the divine necessity that was laid upon him on the path of suffering would also raise him out of the harrowing depths of hell itself—into the glory which he shared with the Father before the world was made (Jn 17:4–5).

The second thing I realize as I face this Scripture is that if Jesus is brought *nearly* to death in the garden of Gethsemane, and is *actually* brought to death on the cross of Calvary, then there is no need for me to be *ultimately* afraid—as if this world were utterly threatening and meaningless. *If* the gospels tell the true story, and *if* the Savior entered into the darkest depths of Gethsemane and Calvary for me, then he gives the lie to all the bleakest and darkest experiences of humankind as the ultimate end.

This does not trivialize the pain, sorrow, and grief of men and women down through the ages, but it does affirm that darkness and chaos are but temporal, and that only love is eternal. It takes the image of God, sweating blood in Gethsemane, pierced through and dying on Calvary, to redeem such atrocities as the Nazi Holocaust, the atomic bombing of Hiroshima and Nagasaki, or Stalin's massacre of ten million human beings. The strong and paradoxical language of Charles Wesley states it precisely:

> *Love divine, what have you done!*
>   *The immortal God has died for me!*
> *The Father's co-eternal Son*
>   *Bore all my sins upon the tree;*
> *The immortal God for me has died!*
>   *My Lord, my Love is crucified—*
>
> *Is crucified for me and you,*
>   *To bring us rebels back to God;*
> *Believe, believe the record true,*
>   *We all are bought with Jesus' blood,*
> *Pardon for all flows from his side:*
>   *My Lord, my Love is crucified.*
>
> *Then let us stand beneath the cross,*
>   *And feel his love a healing stream,*
> *All things for him account but loss,*
>   *And give up all our hearts to him;*
> *Of nothing think or speak beside:*
>   *My Lord, my Love is crucified.*

Exercise

As the evening shadows gather around me tonight, I remember the prayer that I have often prayed with my brothers and sisters and which, when I am alone and enshrouded in darkness, takes on a much deeper and more precise meaning. I would like it to be the prayer on my lips when the angel of death comes to me:

Soul of Christ, sanctify me,
Body of Christ, save me,
Blood of Christ, inebriate me,
Water from the side of Christ, wash me,
Passion of Christ, strengthen me.
O good Jesus, hear me,
Within thy wounds hide me,
Suffer me not to be separated from thee,
From the malicious enemy defend me,
In the hour of my death call me,
And bid me come to thee
That with thy saints I may praise thee
For ever and ever. Amen.

I take some stiff card and slowly and prayerfully make a fair copy of that prayer, reflecting upon its meaning as I write it. Then, taking a candle in a jar, or a torch, I walk out into the darkness that surrounds our earth tonight.

As I walk upon the grass and into the countryside, I remember the garden of Gethsemane, trying to understand the grief and darkness of Jesus as he envisaged the inevitability of his cross. I try to penetrate the meaning of his prayer and of the way he allowed his human will to be brought into complete harmony with the divine will which he recognized as truly his.

He desired human companionship, but there was no one who really understood and entered with him into his interior Gethsemane. He did not want to die, for he was only thirty-three years of age and his human life was a response of love to Love. But in his prayer he said: "*Abba*, Father." The Aramaic word speaks of tender, intimate, strong, paternal love.

He said, "Your will be done" and in saying those words he was not giving up in hopeless submission. He was not beaten into a forced surrender or crying out in anger or frustration. His "*Abba*, Father" meant that he simply let go of anything that was in the way of the Father's perfect will. He let go in compassion, in abandoned obedience, and in simple, childlike trust.

I find a place, sit in the open, surrounded by darkness, with my light burning before me. I center myself in the quietness of the love of God and spend some minutes in silence and darkness, with my flickering light, reflecting on the solitude and compassion of Jesus. Then I open my mind and heart to all those who need my love and prayers tonight, holding them in loving faith before my heavenly Father, quietly saying, "*Abba*, Father, your will be done." I repeat these words over and over until they repeat themselves in my mind and heart.

I stay there for as long as it seems right, and then I shine my light upon the prayer, saying the words slowly, prayerfully, reflecting upon my own darkness and fears, upon my own trust and confidence in God, and upon his grace and love—now and at the hour of my death. I return slowly, savoring my whole meditation and prayer in the light of the garden of Gethsemane.

DAY 6

Trees and Animals

Morning of Day 6: Trees

This morning I hold in my mind's eye the image of a tree. Its roots reach deep down into the humus, drawing sustenance and nourishment from the earth. I feel myself, like that tree, drawing physical and spiritual life from the depths of the Spirit of God. As the sap rises, so in the process of time, foliage, buds, and blossom appear, the limbs and branches reach up and out towards the sunshine and rain. And I pray:

Prayer

Today, my Father, let me be like a tree planted by the river, bringing forth fruit in its season. Let the sap of your Holy Spirit rise within me. Let me not become dry and barren, but rich in abundance and fertility. May many weary ones find refreshment in the shadow of my branches. Through Jesus Christ, the Tree of Life. Amen.

Scripture Reading

Read the following Scripture passages slowly: Genesis 1:29–30; 1 Peter 2:21–25.

Meditation

I remember words of William Blake: "The tree which moves some to tears of joy is in the eyes of others only a green thing which stands in the way."

My room at Glasshampton Monastery is thirty feet above the ground, and for seven summers and six winters I have looked out to the Spanish chestnut tree rising another twenty feet into the sky. I write these words in July, when the tree is heavy with foliage so thick that the threefold division of the main trunk cannot be seen.

During the winter this tree stood stark and bare through frost and cold, through icy rains and bitter winds. In the coming autumn it will bear many thousands of small sweet chestnuts, fit to roast and eat. It is a beautiful tree and it is my friend. I shall always carry the memory of this tree, which speaks to me of the mystery of God and of the spiritual human being. It has borne its dear witness by simply being what it is and has confirmed the truth of those well-loved words of Thomas Merton:

A tree gives glory to God by being a tree. For in being what God means it to be it is obeying Him. It "consents," so to speak, to His creative love. It is expressing an idea which is in God and which is not distinct from the essence of God, and therefore a tree imitates God by being a tree. The more a tree is like itself, the more it is like Him. If it tried to be something else which it was never intended to be, it would be less like God and therefore it would give Him less glory.

I remember as a child seeing a film about an inhabited spacecraft which had been in flight for two or three generations, the original group having left planet Earth because of ecological spoliation. Every evening the flight leader would gather the group in a seated circle, placing upon an easel a large oil painting of a beautiful oak tree in full foliage. They would offer prayer and meditation before it as the symbol of the source of life—an expression of their love and yearning for the earth they had left.

It was an impressionable and moving moment when at last the craft landed upon a renewed earth in blossom and bud. The entire company of men, women, and children trooped out of the craft onto verdant green grass. They were confronted by an immense and fabulous oak tree, far and beyond anything they could have imagined by its painted image. They all fell down before it in a spirit of awe.

Trees have always been for me special messengers and

carriers of the life and presence of God, and the dramatic changes in shape and appearance throughout the changing seasons reflect my own growth in maturity and my changing moods and awareness.

Trees figure prominently in the Bible, for it begins with the Tree of Life in the Garden of Eden and ends with the Tree of Healing in the midst of the Paradise of God. This morning we shall think of some of these trees and discover the way in which theology can become living experience, for all the living images of God in the Bible have their counterpart in the human heart.

First let us look at the Tree of Knowledge of Good and Evil, which is not the same as the Tree of Life. The first few chapters of Genesis are not archeological, geological or biological essays, nor an historical account of how the world came into being. They are *true* but not *literal* accounts of the glory and dilemma of the human situation—what theologians call *existential* accounts, because they are grounded in profound human experience. They have personal, cosmic, and universal significance, as much to do with ecological purity and spoliation as with personal innocence and fall.

We sang a new hymn at the monastery recently, the first part of which expresses all this quite clearly:

> *God who created this Eden of earth,*
> *Giving to Adam and Eve their fresh birth,*
> *What have we done with that wonderful tree?*
> *Lord, forgive Adam,*
> *For Adam is me.*

Adam, ambitious, desires to be wise,
Casts out obedience, then lusts with his eyes;
Grasps his sweet fruit, "As God I shall be,"
  Lord, forgive Adam,
  For Adam is me.

Thirst after power is this sin of my shame,
Pride's ruthless thrust after status and fame,
Turning and stealing and cowering from Thee.
  Lord, forgive Adam,
  For Adam is me.

Cursed is the earth through this
  cancerous crime,
Symbol of man through all passage of time,
Put it all right, Lord; let Adam be free;
  Do it for Adam,
  For Adam is me.

The book of Genesis calls it the Tree of Knowledge of Good and Evil. We can theorize about what human existence would have been like if Adam had not sinned, if we all lived in a state of innocence and communion with God and our fellows. But the fact is that there are trees with rotten roots and bitter fruit. There are also beautiful but poisoned apples like the one which the wicked witch prepared for Snow White—and that also is a powerful symbolic story!

We all thirst for self-knowledge, and it is no accident that "know thyself" was written over the oracle at Delphi, for it reflects the human quest. The lie of the serpent was that by tasting of the forbidden fruit, Adam and Eve could enter into a profound knowledge of themselves and of the mind of God. All that they seem to have *dis-covered* (the word is apt) is a sense of shame at their own nakedness and sexuality. It bears thinking about that the Hebrew word *yadhah*, "to know," has a basic meaning in sexual intercourse and is used in Genesis 4:1—"And Adam *knew* his wife; and she conceived"—and throughout the Bible.

The Genesis story, in line with the biblical tradition, holds human sexuality to be good and wholesome—perhaps the highest function of communion and relationship between men and women. Because of its fundamental sanctity and ecstasy it is capable of becoming a thing of shame to some, and of inordinate and perverted lust to others. Even in some of the great love stories of the world there is the bitter-sweet experience of what has been called postcoital triste—the melancholic sadness which follows upon ecstatic love-making, when the couple can only unite in the flesh while yearning for a consummated unity of being and soul.

Perhaps more than any other human experience—and it is true of all creative acts—human sexuality brings sorrow and pain when separated from the divine Love.

That is not the whole story, of course—we shall discover that in the life-giving tree of the cross. But let us anticipate God's remedy in the final stanzas of the hymn:

> *Glory to God! what is this that I see?*
> *Man made anew, second Adam is he,*
> *Bleeding His love on another fine tree;*
>   *Dies second Adam,*
>   *Young Adam, for me.*

Rises that Adam the master of death,
Pours out His Spirit in holy new breath;
Sheer liberation! With Him I am free!
   Lives second Adam
   In mercy in me.

Now another tree. It is the broom tree found in 1 Kings 19:4, and I call it the Tree of Depression.

Elijah has recently confronted the priests of Baal in the triumphant victory on Mount Carmel and, experiencing the reaction which often comes after victorious testing, he runs off alone into the southern wilderness. There he allows depression to wash over him and finds himself engulfed in fear. This is where he collapses exhausted under the broom tree, which is a bush which grows up to about ten feet and is common in the area south of Beersheba.

Can you see him? He is bunched up, sweating and frustrated, knees up to his chin, tense in body and spirit, filled with fear. Body language communicates a great deal, and Elijah's posture reveals his attitude. His clenched fists, his rapid and shallow breathing, and the uptight inflection of his prayer of complaint show how fouled-up things had become in his mind.

Listen to the prayer as he asks to die: "It is enough; now, O Lord, take away my life; for I am no better than my fathers." The prayer was misguided on all three counts. It was not enough, for the Lord had great work to accomplish through him yet! His life would certainly not be taken away—for a chariot of fire and glory was being prepared for him! And he was certainly better than his fathers, for Elijah the Tishbite is found in Scripture without genealogical table, and no one knows the name of his father!

Things appear distorted to us when we live under the broom tree of depression; and it's not the tree's fault! God's past faithfulness and his own victories seemed to shrink into insignificance when Elijah was faced with Jezebel's fury. Perhaps he was realizing at last that in spite of his triumphalist religion, all was not well within his own soul. Remember that James and John, in their worst religious moments, appealed to this kind of "Elijah triumphalism" when they wanted revenge on the Samaritan village that had rejected Jesus: "Let us call down fire from heaven and consume them—even as Elijah did" (Lk 9:54). Jesus rebuked them! It is interesting to note there are some variant readings in which Elijah's name does not appear, and the rebuke of Jesus is toned down. It looks as if some later editor was embarrassed about the original story! Bad religion is worse than no religion, and bad religion gives rise not only to violence and persecution, but on a personal level to selfish anger and bad temper. Bad temper repressed gives rise to depression—hence Elijah's predicament.

God is gracious in dealing with Elijah, looking first to his physical needs. He hears his complaint and puts him gently to sleep. After a while God's messenger wakes him, providing him with food and drink. These actions are repeated, and then Elijah sets out on a pilgrimage to Mount Horeb where he spends the night in a cave and is then ready for the revelation that God has for him.

Throughout this passage there is a rough honesty and penitence about Elijah's state of soul, which enables God to deal with him at every level of his being. Perhaps depression, anger, and legalistic religion is part of your problem today, and the sleep, food, and rest of this retreat will enable you to be honest and penitent as never before.

Perhaps, too, this is the time to review your sleeping, eating, and drinking habits. Neglect and abuse of the body is to treat the temple of God as an unholy thing. Attention to some of these matters may cause many of your complaints to vanish. Only then will you be enabled to move from the tree of depression to continue the pilgrimage to the cave of the heart on the mount of revelation. Depression need not lead to the downward spiral of despair but to the ascending path to new perspectives in the Lord.

The third tree is the Tree of Conversion, because it gave little Zacchaeus a new perspective on his life and on the person of Jesus—and transformed him in the process. I also like to think of it as a Tree of Curiosity, because Zacchaeus was so eager to see Jesus that instead of being crushed *against* it as an obstacle, he *climbed* it as an instrument of his curiosity. Then the vista of eternity opened up before him. Read the story in Luke 19:1–10.

If you had suggested to Zacchaeus that he should part with some of his ill-gotten gains *before* he climbed the tree, you might have received a sarcastic or cynical reply. It's wonderful what climbing the tree did for him, including the loss of his respectability. Perhaps we should do some curiosity-climbing, opening up our minds and hearts to a new perspective on ourselves and on our Lord!

Elijah's tree of depression depicted an exhausted and frustrated servant of God who had got his religion wrong and needed a renewal of spiritual vision. But Zacchaeus was not caught up in a suicidal depression. He was full of curiosity and was willing to take risks to find some meaning to his life. His job as a tax collector brought him financial success and easy living, but he was lonely, friendless—and perhaps

feeling guilty about his avarice, though he could not acknowledge that until the glory of Jesus shone into his darkened life.

Conversion may not be something that happens only on a
Damascus road with Saul of Tarsus, though it *can* manifest
itself in a sudden and spontaneous turning to God. But how-
ever it happens, it is also a *process* which must transform
the whole of our lives, at every level of our being, and it
takes a lifetime of sanctification to bring it to full fruition.
But we must start somewhere—and the Tree of Curiosity is
a good place to begin!

Exercise

A tree appropriate to our exercise this morning could be
called the Tree of Reflection. It is the fig tree under which
Nathaniel was meditating when Philip, bubbling over with
the joy of his discovery, came to tell him that he had found
Jesus. Meditation under the Tree of Reflection drew Jesus'
attention to Nathaniel, and Nathaniel was amazed when Jesus
told him that he had been looking upon him with the eye of
vision even before Philip called him (Jn 1:45–51). Can you
find such a tree and sit or lean against it, feeling the roots of
your being sinking down into the humus and nourishing
strength of God's Holy Spirit? Can you allow yourself to
reach up toward the heavens, longing for the refreshing sunshine and rain of God's love to embrace you?

In the grounds of the our friary in Dorset, down toward
the woods, you will find a tree planted firmly on the edge of
the path, and an almost life-size wooden figure of Christ
crucified upon it. It is a breathtaking symbol of God's love,

especially if you come upon it suddenly or unexpectedly, and it brings to mind immediately the words of 1 Peter 2:24: "Christ…himself bore our sins in his own body on the tree." This is the Tree of Salvation.

Jesus was a carpenter, and it was redemptively appropriate that he should stretch out his hands and feet upon the tree of the cross, that he should invite the whole world to his wounded heart, that he should expose himself in utter humiliation and love for us poor sinners.

This picture of Christ crucified on a tree of wood portrays the God who is both Creator and Redeemer, for he himself planted the tree on which he was to be crucified. Nature and grace are, therefore, harmoniously brought together in the stark but beautiful image of salvation.

I have an old friend, Sister Pauline, a retired parish worker, who recently wrote to tell me about something that happened to her on a retreat at Glastonbury. This is what she says:

I had never been there before and the talks, the surroundings, the quiet were all so beautiful. One day I walked in the garden where there is a big crucifix in a secluded place. I suddenly came upon it, and sat looking. Yes, I know it's only made of wood, but as I thought and prayed I noticed flies crawling all over it and I began to cry. It seemed like the final, unbearable desecration that the Lord of the Flies should send his emissaries to torment the Lord's sacred body—as if he hadn't suffered enough already. So do you know what I did, dear Ramon—I brushed all the flies away, and kissed the feet of it. Afterwards I was so astonished at

what I had done. Me, the old hard-bitten, true-blue
evangelical.

And she enclosed with the letter her reflection upon the
experience, with which we may conclude our exercise:

> *How could you bear it, Beloved One?...*
> *The noise,*
> *The sneering crowds, ugly-faced and*
>   *fingers pointing;*
> *You who came to tell us of our sweet heritage—*
> *Joint-heirs with you—adopted into the Beloved?*
> *How could you bear it—the nakedness, the shame?*
>
> *How could you bear it, Beloved One?...*
> *The heat,*
> *The screaming nerves and grating bones*
> *As you drew each agonizing breath;*
> *You made the green soft turf, the clear blue sky,*
> *Silvery pampas grass—the gentle breeze*
>   *that stirs my hair.*
> *How could you bear it—the brokenness,*
>   *the pain?*
>
> *How could you bear it, Beloved One?...*
> *The flies,*
> *Emissaries of Beelzebub,*
>   *defiling your holy body,*
> *The final, maddening, inescapable,*
>   *insulting malevolence!*
> *How could you bear it, O my sweet Lord?*

It was the flies that broke my heart;
Yes, I am brave in adversity;
Life's hammer-blows do not daunt me
Undergirded by your strong love...
But the pin-pricks, the petty irritations,
The things that harass my spirit,
    spin in my mind,
Ruffle my peace...
O sweet Jesus—help me to remember the flies...

Meal Preparation for
DAY 6

Colcannon

4 medium-sized potatoes, peeled and chopped
2 large carrots, very thinly sliced
1/2 medium turnip, cut into small chunks
1 large parsnip, cut into small pieces (remove
    woody center)
salt and pepper to taste
2 to 4 ozs margarine or butter

Any combination of root vegetables can be cooked together in a large pan until soft, then strained thoroughly.
Mash with plenty of margarine or butter, and season
with salt and pepper.

This can be served with green vegetables, baked beans,
or poached eggs—or just enjoyed on its own.

Evening of Day 6: Animals

One of the most popular stories of Saint Francis is his taming of the wolf of Gubbio. The wolf infected the townspeople with terror and hatred. Francis went alone into the woods, faced the wolf, reasoned with him, and entered into such a communicative cooperation that wolf and people lived in an harmonious relationship from that time onward.

It is a story for today, for there is a new awareness of our relationship with and dependence upon the animal world. Christians should be in the forefront of animal husbandry and care, opposing animal abuse and cruelty at every level and supporting all agencies of positive help and research. The following words by Walt Whitman border on the sentimental but they have always moved me:

> *I think I could turn and live with animals,*
> *   they are so placid and self-contained,*
> *I stand and look at them long and long.*
> *They do not sweat and whine about their condition,*
> *They do not lie awake in the dark and weep*
> *   for their sins,*
> *They do not make me sick discussing*
> *   their duty to God,*
> *Not one is dissatisfied, not one is demented*
> *   with the mania of owning things,*
> *Not one kneels to another, nor to his kind that*
> *   lived thousands of years ago,*
> *Not one is respectable or industrious*
> *   over the whole earth.*

Prayer

Heavenly Father: Thank you for the variety and vitality of the animal creation. Forgive us that we so often use them only as beasts of burden and victims of our own will. As far as lies in us, help us to live together with your creatures in harmony and gratitude, for you love them as you love us. Through Jesus Christ, our Lord. Amen.

Scripture Reading

Read the following Scripture passages slowly: Genesis 20–25; Numbers 22:21–35; Luke 19:28–38.

Meditation

This coming Sunday scores of horses and their riders will ride past Glasshampton Monastery for charity. Around the monastery there are foxes, badgers, stoats, squirrels, pheasants, and partridges. The cuckoo sounds in my ears as I write these words and I have a list before me, compiled by one of our retreatants, of fifty-five species of bird life around Glasshampton, beginning with a gray heron and ending with a yellowhammer.

During your retreat you may like to explore the animal life of your area in an attitude of prayerful mindfulness. But just now I want to restrict our meditation to two species— the dog and the donkey. The dog may not be everyone's animal, but it is certainly mine, which is represented by Susie and Mungo. Susie was the Cardiganshire corgi I owned in my first years in the ministry. She died years ago, but her memory still brings me to tears for all she represents. She was loving, gentle, devoted, and sensitive. Mungo is the present monastery dog—half spaniel and half red setter—full of joy, energy, and a ministering animal to guests and friars alike.

The donkey is represented by Jacomena, the one-time resident in our Dorset friary, and now retired to the Dorset Donkey Sanctuary, and by Balaam's ass in the Old Testament, and by the donkey from Bethany in the New.

These are the animals through whom I have seen, touched, and experienced the love and grace of God—images of nature on the road to heaven.

First of all, Susie. Why does she bring me to tears? I think it is because of the memory of her complete canine devotion and trust. Any word of rebuke would hurt her deeply, any change of mood would be recognized, and every look of love and affection would cause her to tremble with ecstasy. What can one do in the face of love like that? It is the kind of love which children and the young of every species can stimulate in those around them. In Susie there was no malice or treachery, no harboring of resentments, but only forgiveness, fidelity, and affection.

And Mungo! Well, he is loving and joyful and faithful, too. But his ministry at Glasshampton embraces the healing of wounds and the absorption of pain. One of our guests said recently that Mungo bears a great deal of the sadness and conflict that surrounds him in this beautiful and healing place. Guests come with their joys and sorrows, novices work through great conflicts with vocation and together with the other friars enter into the life of prayer and the finitude of our vulnerable lives. Time and again Mungo seems to understand, to enter into individual and corporate pain, ministering in his own way as a creature of God, bearing grace and healing.

Last year a guest came to Glasshampton in great heaviness at the breakdown of his marriage. As he sat on the round brick flowerbed in the garth in dejection and loneliness, Mungo came out during the evening prayer time, quietly jumped on the low wall, put his head into the guest's lap. The guest wrote to me after his return home, "Mungo just understood my loneliness and pain." He also enclosed a check for Mungo!

Mungo is not as meltingly loving or unreservedly trusting as Susie was, but he has a wisdom, a canniness, a playful mischief, which enables him to keep his end up when swamped by guests, visitors, and brothers of all temperaments—him being the only specimen of the canine species!

He has had sermons preached about him, an article on him in the *Church Times* (for which he received an honorarium that went to pay for dog food), and honorable mentions in publications, prayer schools, and retreats.

Jacomena. She was the donkey, said to be thirty-three years old when I first became acquainted with her. She had a reputation for being nasty, cantankerous, and dangerous. I was told that she had bitten the hand of the fellow who came to trim her hooves. If you went too near her (and I proved this!), she would turn and give you a kick, her two back legs frisking into the air.

Then I read an article on donkeys that said if they are left alone they can become crotchety and nasty, but if you bring them into company and show affection for them they can become manageable, companionable, and even lovable.

So I tried it. I went down to the lonely field, untethered

Jacomena, and brought her into the friary grounds. I took her down into the graveyard where she cropped the grass, and I spent time with her, talking, patting, feeding, and playing with her.

Then one day, in the same graveyard, I was talking and chuckling to her and playing the game that we had invented. I would make a little run towards her and she would suddenly run aside and dodge me. Then she would make a run toward me and I would do the same. We had perfected this into a secret game between us—she would rarely do it if there were others about.

Then suddenly, I lay upon the grass on my back, put my legs into the air and shouted, "Hey Jacomena, come and play!" She looked somewhat disdainfully at me (I often felt she thought me a bit daft) and then lay down on her back and kicked her legs in the air—just as I was doing.

That really heralded the change of mood. She became friendly and docile (mostly!) with the children, enjoyed tidbits, and especially digestive cookies. Benedict and Rameen cared for her after me, and Nobby Clark took her for walks around the perimeter of the friary.

One summer the flies attacked the small infection around her eyes and we gently, carefully, persistently treated it with ointment and powder, and she let us do it.

When I meet Benedict and Rameen we still talk about her—nearly ten years later. And I look at two beautiful pictures I have of her—one in the rosy and pink evening, looking endearing, and the other pulling at the end of her long tether, wide-open mouth braying for attention and a game. I hope she is happy among the other donkeys as an old lady now in the Donkey Sanctuary.

I didn't have to be religious to be near God when I played with Jacomena. The rough cross on her back reminded me of Chesterton's poem which I loved as a boy, called "The Donkey":

> *When fishes flew and forests walked*
>   *And figs grew upon thorn,*
> *Some moment when the moon was blood*
>   *Then surely I was born;*
>
> *With monstrous head and sickening cry*
>   *And ears like errant wings,*
> *The devil's walking parody*
>   *On all four-footed things;*
>
> *The tattered outlaw of the earth*
>   *Of ancient crooked will;*
> *Starve, scourge, deride me: I am dumb,*
>   *I keep my secret still.*
>
> *Fools! For I also had my hour;*
>   *One far fierce hour and sweet:*
> *There was a shout about my ears,*
>   *And palms before my feet.*

I can feel for that donkey. Reading it again I remember my first emotional and boyish response to it. What did it matter that the shape seemed lopsided, that people laughed at the hee-haw sound, or that it was starved, scourged, and derided? Jesus looked upon it, loved it, chose it, needed it, and rode upon it.

And that brings us this evening to Balaam's ass. This is a

primitive story I've always loved, reflecting the Semites' regard for the donkey as credited with intuitive insight. My experience with Jacomena gave me some insight into the nature of a donkey and taught me that when I treat my fellow-creatures (subrational or human) with kindness and creaturely appreciation, then I receive a response of friendship and joy. Balaam learned the hard way!

Balaam was a seer and ought to have known better. His mind was full of the religious problems of blessing and cursing. He would have been better off if he had laid aside his philosophical reflection on the will of God as he went his way, and taken heed to his insightful donkey. The angel of the Lord blocked his way but only the donkey saw it. Three times this happened, and each time the donkey turned aside and was beaten by the insensitive Balaam.

At last the donkey fell down before the angel, and Balaam beat her with his staff. Then the amazing thing happened. We read that "the Lord opened the mouth of the donkey and she said to Balaam, 'What have I done to you that you have struck me these three times?'" Then follows a dialogue in which the donkey shows herself to be wiser than her master, and as a result of which Balaam's eyes are opened to the angel standing sword in hand—and the truth dawns forcefully upon him.

Don't worry about the frankly supernatural garb of the story. I believe that the Lord who shut the mouths of the lions in the Daniel story can open the mouth of the donkey in the Balaam story. The fact is that angelic ministry is sent sometimes to open up the way and sometimes to block the way in our lives. Frequently we are too cerebral to discern it, or we are working out our own religious accommodations to an unbelieving world so that we shall not lose face or be accused of being an ass!

I wonder if the Bethany donkey which carried Jesus was a distant descendant of this one? And if God cares for and uses such creatures, will he not use me?

I did not intend to introduce another creature, but I've just finished Ted Simon's book *Jupiter's Travels*, in which he describes his incredible four years' adventure around the world on a motor bike. He is in India, climbing from Kerala to Dotacamund, describing the silvery gray monkeys with long furry limbs jumping among the tall groves of areca palms. I am struck with the way in which Ted, with no religion, but profoundly impressed with the sacred spirit of India, writes of these monkeys and of himself:

They seemed so close to enlightenment, as though at any moment they might stumble over it and explode into consciousness. Their curiosity is extreme. They experiment with any unfamiliar object, a coin, a hat, a piece of paper, just as a human baby does, pulling it, rubbing it, sticking it in their ears, hitting it against other things. And nothing comes of it. To be so close, yet never to pierce the veil!

I looked at myself in the same light, as a monkey given my life to play with, prodding it, trying to stretch it into different shapes, dropping it, and picking it up again, suspecting always that it must have some use and meaning, tantalized, and frustrated by it but always unable to make sense of it....A latent power of perception was stirring in me.

Dogs and donkeys and monkeys. The ways of God are strange—and beautiful!

Exercise

If you have field glasses with you this week, take them and seek out an animal or bird this evening. Or go and look at a horse, some cattle or sheep, and learn from the animal creation. Perhaps you ought to obtain some factual information about the care, preservation, and misuse of animals by humans. Why not actually do something for them, in the alleviation of animal suffering, or offering time, money, or help to some society involved in such work?

Once you begin such research and discovery you will be appalled at the suffering of some animals and encouraged by the dedication of those people who seek to ease that suffering.

DAY 7

Sabbath and Paradise

Morning of Day 7: The Sabbath

"The sabbath is made for people and not people for the sabbath" (Mk 2:27). This is a liberating text that is meant to free us from a legalistic and constricting religion into the freedom of the children of God.

I was always perplexed, first as a young Christian and then as a minister and priest, to find that some Christians exhausted themselves on their sabbath by organizing and participating in endless services, meetings, rallies, and various other circuses. At the end of the day, instead of being refreshed by worship and attendance upon God's word and

sacrament, and collected in heart and mind, ready for the
week's labor and service, they were distracted and tired out
in body and mind, having forgotten the biblical principle of
sabbath observance.

Christians don't keep the Saturday sabbath of the old cov-
enant, but observe the resurrection Sunday of the new, with
its emphasis upon new life, joy, and freedom. Nevertheless,
the principle of a one-day-in-seven rest from labor must not
be lost. This is part of the creative and restorative process
which God intends for all people in order that they may "rest
in the Lord and wait patiently for him." In this way his tranquillity and recuperative healing power will flow through
us to other lives.

Prayer

God of creation and Lord of the sabbath: You created the
heavens and the earth and rested on the seventh day. You
commanded your ancient people to cease from their work
and rest in your love. Save us from our frenetic activities
and enable us to let go our neurotic anxieties. Reveal to us
your glory that we may gaze upon your beauty and be filled
with your love. Through Jesus Christ, our Lord. Amen.

Scripture Reading

Read the following Scripture passages slowly: Exodus 20:8–
11; Luke 13:10–17; Hebrews 4:1–11.

Meditation

After the six days of creation, God entered into rest. The sabbath is not, therefore, a legalistic commandment binding God's people to a moralistic duty, but a principle of leisure, freedom, worship, and praise. On the sabbath day (or week or month or year), we are freed from the ordinary work and anxiety that surround us in order that we may engage ourselves creatively in worship, meditation, and all the restorative activities that renew and refresh our spiritual, mental, and physical lives.

It is especially sad when I find clergy and professional people who have been granted some months of sabbatical leave, after years of duty, using the period as a means of exhaustive academic or promotional work, which leaves them with no time for God, for their families, or themselves.

But I am gladdened and refreshed when I find others planning their sabbatical leave with relaxation, personal and family leisure, and creative spiritual or academic pursuits, which refresh and relax them for immersion again into the busy world as more centered and spiritual people.

We live in a busy world, and Christians are often among the busiest people. In the midst of a busy family with a demanding financial lifestyle, the principle of sabbath is increasingly difficult to observe, whether that means a day in a week, or periods of days, when mother, father, and children are free to spend time alone with God or in simple, relaxing joy with one another. It may be necessary for us to review our idea of sabbath, leading us to simplify our lifestyle, drop some commitments, cut down on our spendthrift socializing, and learn to be quiet. Perhaps we are worrying and working ourselves into gastric, circulatory, or cardiac illness—and premature death!

I'm not advocating a legalistic sabbath observance! I well remember the kind of Sunday when the TV had a cloth draped over it (though that was not such a bad thing!), and we were not encouraged to take public transport, buy Sunday newspapers (or buy anything), ride a bicycle, or go for a swim. Though for some reason, the woman of the house was expected to cook a larger lunch and dessert than on other days of the week! Such attitudes were enjoined on every member of the congregation, and although some of the negative "don'ts" have been dropped, there seems to be an increase in religious activity and organized observances.

It can be something of an eyeopener, therefore, when a congregation takes off together for the weekend, so that the Saturday or Sunday looks something like this:

8:00 A.M.	Eucharist and meditation
9:00 A.M.	Communal breakfast
10:00 A.M.	Family Eucharist (for those not at 8:00 A.M.); supervised childcare until lunch to give parents a rest
1:00 P.M.	Communal lunch
3:00 P.M.	Voluntary leisure activities, including walking, swimming, games, painting, music making, poetry reading, social groups, reading
5:00 P.M.	Light meal and evensong
7:30 P.M.	Communal meal

8:30 P.M.   Led meditation with music and silence,
             leading into Compline at about 9:30 P.M.
             Post-Compline Silence encouraged,
             though individuals free to talk/share
             without interrupting community silence.

The value of a weekend like this is to ensure that the family groups have rest from children, and the young singles and older people share in the child-minding—providing quiet, recreation, and creative activities for all.

Moving from the group to the personal, the sabbath principle is that as the divine pattern is a day's rest in seven, so the creation should observe a like sabbath. It applies to the land, where fields are allowed to lie fallow, to animals, who have their day's rest, as well as to all levels of society. If the busy businessperson, teacher, doctor, nurse, artisan, manual worker, and scholar observed such a principle, our society would be the better for it, whatever day of the week was observed.

If in the Christian congregation there was a commitment to baby-minding, childcare, and sick-care, then everyone could participate on a regular basis. It is not idleness that is being advocated, but leisure—freedom from the daily demands that drain us of imaginative energy.

In the story of the healing of the crippled woman, Jesus was not idle, but creatively active on the sabbath, though criticized by the legalistic, hypocritical church members around him. He observed the principle of sabbath by a dynamic healing ministry, liberating the woman from the bondage of Satan and debilitating sickness into the sabbath freedom of praise and health. The result of the sabbath healing was that "all his adversaries were put to shame; and all the people rejoiced at all the glorious things that were done by him."

Jesus observed his sabbath not only by synagogue worship and compassionate works of healing, but by spending time alone in the wilderness, on the mountain, early in the morning or through the night. Then he offered rest to others: "Come to me, all who labor and are heavy laden, and I will give you rest" (Mt 11:28).

It seems superfluous to encourage Christians to rest, to wait upon the Lord, to learn simple methods of relaxation and meditation. Such practices should be basic to their discipleship; such contemplative waiting should be the soil within which their life of service is rooted. More often than not they suffer from the same workaholic diseases as many ambition-hungry worldlings.

On the other hand there are those in our society who have been made redundant or who cannot find productive and satisfying work who have become *idle*, not able to appreciate or use their enforced leisure because it spells out rejection to them.

Both these groups need to cultivate a method of meditation, which includes relaxation, alertness, and the use of the mind and heart in resting in God. This lies at the heart of our simple centering method at the beginning of this book, which includes (1) resting, (2) breathing, and (3) opening.

When the Christian faith consists of theological opinions and good works alone (though both are necessary) but omits the practice of prayer and meditation, it becomes simply a philosophy of life among others, and its proponents become at worst convert-hunters, proselytizers, and sheep-stealers, and at best perpetrators of a moralistic system of ethics and charity.

Christian faith has to do with forgiveness, healing, salvation, reconciliation, justice, equality, and a deepening awareness of the dynamic life of God flowing through his people. Therefore the practice of prayer and meditation is indispensable to the communal and personal life of the believer. It may be that it is the neglect of this sabbath principle which is at the root of much of our Western Christian malaise. We cannot work effectively because we cannot rest.

Exercise

After centering down, turn in your Bible to the healing of the crippled woman in Luke 13:10–17 and let your mind and heart be open to the attitude of Christ to the sabbath. This passage shows him using the day to gather with the faithful people for worship, and teaching the sacred word to the congregation.

Visualize the scene as he sees the poor woman bent double among the listeners. Compassion wells up in his heart as he feels her bondage to an alien spirit, and he cries out with boldness and faith: "Woman, you are free from your infirmity." Then he goes over to her, lays his hands upon her, and her spine straightens and she stands erect and gives praise to God.

Here is Jesus, uninhibited about his faith and open to the springs of human compassion, liberated from a legalistic keeping of external sabbath regulations. For him, human need comes before ritualistic rules, and the religious synagogue officials become angry because he offended against the rule book, though not against the spirit of the law. When they upbraided him he affirmed the priority of human need over sabbath rules, and saw it wholly appropriate that this "daughter of Abraham" should be set free from the bondage of the devil on such a day as this. His answer was so clear, powerful, and anointed that the religionists were put to shame by it. But the people rejoiced because of the wonderful things that he was doing.

If the result of our religious practices were to release such a spirit of forgiveness, compassion, and healing, then the witness of our lives would bring hope and faith to many ordinary people.

Stay with this passage in meditation and feel yourself to be set free and straightened as the woman was. Let the sabbath principle be to you one of liberation and resting in the love of God. And ask that the influence of your witness may be that the enemies of love may be ashamed and that the common people may rejoice.

Vegetable Ragout

8 ozs sliced onions
2 Tbsps oil
1 large sweet pepper, sliced (green or red)
8 ozs carrots, sliced
1/2 small cauliflower head, divided into florets
   or 8 ozs mushrooms, sliced, *or* other
   vegetables according to season
8 ozs fresh tomatoes or canned
garlic to taste
salt and pepper to taste

In a pan, sauté the onions until soft, but not brown. Add the other vegetables, except tomatoes. Cover and simmer until soft. Add tomatoes, salt, pepper, garlic, and other herbs, if available. Serve with rice and cucumber raita.

Cucumber Raita

Cut half a cucumber into very thin matchsticks. Add these to a small tub of natural yogurt with a squeeze of lemon, plus half a clove of crushed garlic.

Evening of Day 7:Paradise

It is difficult for the human mind to speak of God, to communicate any experience of the divine to others in word or image. But we must use words, and we must employ images, analogies, metaphors, parables, to try to convey something of the spiritual dimension that moves us to joy, that meets us in forgiveness, that stirs and challenges us to reach out in compassion. One of the most difficult areas of which to speak in these days is that which deals with the future life—the language of heaven. We do realize that the Bible uses images and analogies, employing human language to communicate spiritual and divine experience and truth, but we must beware of an overliteral interpretation of symbolic passages, yet hold to the inward truth of what is revealed.

Prayer

God our Father: You have prepared for those who love you a heavenly abode and kingdom which eye has not seen, nor ear heard, nor heart understood. Help us to reach within and beyond the poor language which limits the heavenly realm to earthly symbols; grant us the gift of your Holy Spirit that we may grasp the inward truth of your indwelling, both here and in eternity. Through Jesus Christ, our Lord. Amen.

Scripture Reading

Read the following Scripture passages slowly: Genesis 28:10–19; Revelation 21:22–25.

Meditation

I was brought up on what is now called anthropomorphic language (from *anthropos* = man, and *morphe* = form or shape). That means speaking of the being of God in the form or shape of a human being. For instance, "The *eye* of the Lord is upon the righteous and his *ear* is open to their cry," or "The *arm* of the Lord is not shortened that it cannot save, neither is his *ear* heavy that it cannot hear." I learned that Christ is *seated* at the right *hand* of the Father on his *throne* in heaven—and many other things that are true, yet symbolic. For I know that God has no body, parts, or passions, does not have eyes, ears, tongue, hands, or feet. He has no right hand, nor does he sit, therefore he does not need a throne, and heaven is not up there or out there or *anywhere* at all, for it is not a geographical or spatial location. And yet all the language is true, though not literal fact.

I was fortunate enough to realize this, through good teaching and an early introduction to the Greek Fathers of the Church. But I have known former childhood friends who have rejected the whole package of Christian belief because they were taught, and could no longer believe, the literal image of Jesus as "above in a bright, blue sky."

And as well as a Friend, there's a palm, a robe, a harp, a crown, and so on. I learned that these things were true, though not literal—my friends didn't make it!

There is a great deal of analogy and imagery in the story of Jacob's ladder, which symbolizes commerce between heaven and earth. As well as ascending and descending angels, Jacob perceives God as up there, on top of the ladder, in heaven. God communicates his revelation to Jacob, and when he wakes from his dream his words are significant: "Surely the Lord is in this place; and I did not know it." And he was afraid and said, "How awesome is this place! This is none other than the house of God *(Beth El)*, and this is the gate of heaven." Then he erected a pillar and anointed it with oil to mark it as a holy place.

By the new name, Bethel, God's people remembered that *this was the place* where God spoke with the patriarch, and such places become holy sites of pilgrimage, suffused with the glory of the presence of that primordial revelation. Heaven is here. Here is the place where one enters heaven—this is the gateway into the new dimension, into the eternal world, for heaven has broken through here.

The world's stories are full of such hidden and secret gateways—every literate child knows C. S. Lewis's *The Lion, the Witch, and the Wardrobe*, and that the gateway into Narnia was discovered by Lucy in the back of an old wardrobe—a most unlikely place. For Narnia, like heaven, is more a dimension than a location.

So if heaven is the place of the redeemed it need not be locational (though, of course, it *could* be if God so caused it to be). But none of this is new. Much of it was understood by the biblical writers themselves, and the Fathers and Mothers of the Church were well acquainted with symbolical and allegorical writing and interpretation. But we must use the language of the "here and now" to communicate the truth of the "there and then." We don't have any other language.

So when we speak of heaven as a garden or a city, with golden or bejewelled gates, pavements of gold, walls of jasper, a sea of glass, with saints in white garments and palms, with golden crowns on their heads and harps in their hands, we are using allegorical or metaphorical language to convey the preciousness, the glory, the harmony, the security, and the dazzling wonder of the life of the world to come.

Heaven is *now*, the kingdom of God is within the heart, and the prophetic tradition that speaks of the holy mountain where the lion shall lie down with the lamb and a little child shall lead them is trying to speak of the restoration of the old symbolic Eden. The joy of living together in harmony and peace is conveyed by saying that "they shall beat their swords into plowshares and their spears into pruning hooks."

That may sound naive, but it actually states the inwardness of things. It means that the true wealth of the soul is not found in the accumulation of earthly riches or the achieving of human ambition or reputation. It is the purity of heart that comes from a simple life lived in compassion. This is what will last through death, and what Jesus meant when he said: "Lay not up for yourselves treasures on earth, where moth and rust corrupt and thieves break through and steal, but lay up for yourselves treasure in heaven...for where your treasure is, there will your heart be also" (Mt 6:19–21).

This gives real meaning to the simple and poor life of Jesus on earth, and of Saint Francis of Assisi, his most literal follower, for he knew what things to take literally. God does not promise a pact of plenty to those who follow and love him—rather poverty, persecution, hardship, and sometimes torture and death. The whole gospel bears witness to such a life, and the eleventh chapter of the book of Hebrews shows men and women who lived that life as looking for a city and a country whose foundations are in heaven, with a test and a reward of love which is far and above anything that can be hoped for upon earth.

None of that indicates that we are to allow the poor to be oppressed on earth or that we should approve of injustice, inequality, or the treading down of minorities. Rather, imbued with the values and virtues of the kingdom of God (see Sermon on the Mount in Mt 5–7), and anointed by the Spirit of God, we should seek for God's will to be done on earth as it is in heaven. We should, therefore, be careful in interpreting such apocalyptic books as Daniel and the Revelation, for they are full of figures, analogies, prophetic, and apocalyptic symbolism and natural and earthly metaphors to convey heavenly and spiritual realities.

If we fail to do this we shall start, as some have done, to dig ourselves in before the nuclear battle of Armageddon, with stockpiled foodstuffs guarded with guns and ammunition, or we shall start climbing mountains on a set date to greet the Second Coming of Christ, or interpret certain secret and coded language in the apocalyptic books to be fulfilled before our very eyes in the person of any contemporary political tyrant. Of course the antichrist *may* be prefigured by Nero, Attila the Hun, Napoleon, Hitler, Stalin, or whatever oppressor may hold contrary political views to our own—but to see history laid out in the apocalyptic books as a plain blueprint which only *our* eyes can see is to fall into an old heresy. None of this is new. It was already an abuse in the New Testament Church and can be illustrated throughout history, including the apocalyptic visions of some of the political *zelanti* Franciscan friars of the thirteenth century and right down to our own day.

In the light of all this, there are certain guidelines for interpretation. First it is necessary to read the Scriptures intelligently, in a prayerful spirit of openness. Then it is wise to read "with the Church," inquiring what the great people of faith have written and said about particular passages, not interpreting Scripture privately.

There are negative and positive values in this. Negatively, you will be saved from historical and theological heresy and from a naive literal fundamentalism. Positively, you will be set free to value the varied interpretations of the fathers and mystics and be able to see the communal and personal value of Scripture on your own pilgrimage of faith.

When we endeavor to understand the nature of heaven or paradise as beginning *now* within the experience of the loving relationship of people as the Body of Christ, or within the blessedness of personal spiritual experience, we can relate it to the *practice* of spirituality. What I mean by that is that we can have a *foretaste* of the glory to come by participating *now* in love, in worship, in adoration, in contemplative prayer.

When people are in love they are taken out of themselves (this is what the word *ecstasy* means) into a new sphere of personal and shared relationship—a kind of heaven on earth. When a person enters into the reality of prayer, either communally in the Eucharist or in personal/shared contemplative prayer, there is a longing satisfied, and a yearning stimulated for its fullness in heaven.

Although it is difficult or impossible for us to imagine the utterly new dimension we call heaven, or to think of life outside our present body or clothed with an immortal body, it is significant that the New Testament descriptions of the ways which only the spiritual mind can glimpse on earth.

And the spiritual mind is one in which the whole being is given to God in love and to our fellow human beings in loving service, thus fulfilling the two great commandments.

Thus, in looking forward to the glories of the life to come, we can negate the sorrow, pain, and sin of earth and affirm all that is good and true and beautiful within the love of God. Thomas à Kempis in his hymn on heaven, *Jerusalem Luminosa*, has a vision of the transfiguration of the mortal after the pattern of the Transfiguration and Resurrection of Jesus, as he writes:

> *O how glorious and resplendent*
>   *Fragile body, shalt thou be,*
> *When endowed with so much beauty,*
>   *Full of health, and strong, and free,*
> *Full of vigor, full of pleasure*
>   *That shall last eternally.*

Exercise

We have seen that heaven on earth may be anticipated in various ways. One of the primary ways is prayer, and especially the Church's prayer around the altar of God in holy Communion. An important aspect of the life of prayer is the cultivation of a personal contemplation of the being and love of God and of a realization of his presence in your own experience. This is something that can be practiced especially in retreat, rooted in Scripture and in the quiet waiting upon the Spirit of God.

This evening, after the centering down method, use the following material and allow the Lord to lead your meditation into interior stillness.

1. Anticipate the joy and harmony of heaven by reflection upon the two great commandments: (a) you shall love the Lord your God with all your heart, soul, mind, and strength; (b) you shall love your neighbor as yourself.

2. Anticipate the reconciling union of heaven by a present awareness of the communion of saints, affirming that you will be one with the whole Body of Christ in the fellowship of love. This will include all the great saints of all time, all the equally loved but little-known people of God, and your loved ones in Christ who have gone before.

3. Realize that all that is of God's creative love on earth will not be lost but transfigured and enjoyed in heaven.

In the light of this meditation, see how the humblest things of earth can become the very experience of heaven in this poem by Mary Elizabeth Coleridge, noting also how in the eternal realm the first shall be last and the last first, in a divine reversal:

> *As Christ the Lord was passing by,*
> *He came, one night, to a cottage door.*
> *He came, a poor man, to the poor;*
> *He had no bed whereon to lie.*
>
> *He asked in vain for a crust of bread,*
> *Standing there in the frozen blast.*
> *The door was locked and bolted fast.*
> *"Only a beggar!" the poor man said.*

Christ the Lord went further on,
    Until He came to a palace gate.
    There a king was keeping his state,
In every window the candles shone.

The king beheld Him out in the cold.
    He left his guests in the banquet-hall.
    He bade his servants tend them all.
"I wait on a Guest I know of old."

"'Tis only a beggar-man!" they said.
    "Yes," he said, "It is Christ the Lord."
    He spoke to Him a kindly word,
He gave Him wine and he gave Him bread.

Now Christ is Lord of Heaven and Hell,
    And all the words of Christ are true.
    He touched the cottage, and it grew;
He touched the palace, and it fell.

The poor man is become a king.
    Never a man so sad as he.
    Sorrow and Sin on the throne make three,
He has no joy in mortal thing.

But the sun streams in at the cottage door
    That stands where once the palace stood.
    And the workman, toiling to earn his food,
Was never a king before.

PART 4

CREATION-CENTERED AND REDEMPTION-CENTERED SPIRITUALITY

Creation-Centered and Redemption-Centered Spirituality

THERE HAS BEEN A SHIFT in emphasis over the last decade or two in the whole area of spirituality. If I think of this as the swing of a pendulum, then the swing has been away from redemption and towards creation. The positive value of such an analogy is that the pendulum swings are rhythmic and constant in regularity, and only thus will the clock-face indicate the truth. But all such mechanical analogies break down, for both creation and redemption indicate a living reality. Creation indicates the initiating, creative-sustaining power of God in a living organism, and redemption indicates the redeeming and reconciling love which gives itself even to suffering and death in the healing of the world's wounds. That is why this book draws on nature *and* grace, creation *and* redemption, in pointing us to the Love, which is at the heart of all things.

As the catholic and evangelical sections of the Church must mingle and share their particular emphases in theology and spirituality, so there must be a mingling of the creative and redemptive aspects of spirituality, reflecting a biblical faith for all the people of God.

If creation is emphasized to the detriment of redemption, this may result in a sentimental natural theology, which takes no account of the exceeding sinfulness of sin. Thus, because of an inability to diagnose the profound sickness of our fallen humanity, a merely therapeutic plaster is placed on to a pernicious suppurating wound in an attempt to hide the terminal sickness unto death, which infects the body of the human race.

Another danger may result from an espousal of all kinds of "new age" spiritualities, which embrace spiritist cults of a syncretistic kind, practicing esoteric forms of fertility rites, or flirting with erotic forms of sensuality, which may lead to an abuse and not an affirmation of human sexuality. There is nothing new in all this, of course—the Church has faced gnosticisms and fertility religions before—but these are syncretistic days and discernment has to be exercised.

But if redemption is emphasized to the detriment of creation, then the Church may become obsessed with the Fall in the book of Genesis, instead of first affirming the goodness of creation in that narrative, as it came from the hand of God. This leads to such dark doctrines of sin that lead to an *absolute* rupture between man and God, so that the divine image is not only broken, defaced, or damaged (which it is!) but utterly lost, leaving no continuity or relation at all between man and God. Such dark doctrines spill over into redemption, so that human sexuality and creativity are suspect at root level, and creation is so fallen that it cannot reflect anything of the divine presence or love.

It is dangerous to be simplistic, but it is fairly true to say that the emphasis in the Eastern Orthodox Churches has been on a creation-centered spirituality, viewing sin in terms of the sickness of an organism needing the healing power of the Savior. In this view the Eucharist is the "medicine of immortality" and redemption is understood in Athanasian terms as *theosis*, or the divinization of our humanity. We become partakers of the divine nature.

In the Western or Latin Church the emphasis has been on the legalistic and forensic nature of sin as the breaking of God's law, with a consequent punitive banishment from the divine presence, leading to a view, at worst, of humankind as massa perditionis—a universal mass or lump of damnation—sin being propagated from parent to child by the physical act of generation.

It would be quite wrong to set the Greek and Latin Fathers in opposition, and if the above paragraphs are a simplistic generalization they state the extreme emphases in order to make the point. The main thrust of what I am saying is that we need to see that innocence, righteousness, and love are basic to creation—paradise came before the fall! Therefore we are made for love, and in spite of the dreadful and universal reality of our fallenness and need for redemption, God's presence and mercy can be traced in creation and in our human nature.

Because of the alienation and rupture in our relationship with God we need redemption—and that is why the cross is planted in the midst of the world. The cross cannot be bypassed.

The Creator-God became the Redeemer-God to bridge the chasm, heal the wound, fulfill the law of love, and take us into his redemptive embrace. "The lamb was slain before the foundation of the world," and the Scripture which relates most wonderfully the Creator-Redeemer is 2 Corinthians 5:19: "God was in Christ reconciling the world to himself."

It is only the redeemed sinner who can see God clearly in his creation, and the main thrust of this book is to lead the retreatant more deeply into an experience of the redeeming God in the works of nature. Both the glory and the pain of our redemption can be traced in nature and reflected in Scripture. The changing of the seasons not only reveals our finitude and mortality but holds out the promise of eternal life and immortality through the redeeming love of the God who created us, the Christ who died for us and the Spirit who indwells us and saturates the whole of creation with his life-giving breath.

If these days have been spent in the loving presence of God, in the experience of prayerful meditation upon the themes of nature and grace, then it will have been a glimpse of heaven on earth and an affirmation of all the riches of the God who made us in his image and redeemed us by his love. These two aspects of God's loving character are brought together in Scripture and in the Church's liturgy, and at the end of our retreat it would be an excellent exercise for us to write out on index cards these two quotations so that we might carry them and learn them by heart. They will bring us "down the mountain," allowing the radiance of the Transfiguration to shine in our daily lives. The first is from the Second Letter to the Corinthians (4:6), and the second from the prayer at the mingling of the wine and water at the Eucharist:

The God who said, "Let light shine out of darkness" has shone in our hearts to give the light of the knowledge of the glory of God in the face of Jesus Christ.

O God, not only have you, in fashioning human nature, given it marvelous gifts, but you have even more marvelously redeemed it. Grant that, through the mystery of the mingling of this water and wine, we may be made partakers of the divinity of him who became a partaker of our humanity, Jesus Christ, your Son, our Lord. Amen.